MW01603052

RA PRESS

100 Kennedy Drive #53

South Burlington, VT. 05403

ISBN 978-1-365-49085-9

TAKING ON GLOBAL HEALTH ISSUES

ODYSSEY of a DEVELOPMENTAL PEDIATRICIAN

Dr. Alfred Scherzer

To Joan with Love
Al
1/6/17

DEDICATION

To my daughters Lisa, Andrea, and Martha whose separate and divergent lives mirror their fierce independence; and to my loving partner, Debbie, who has given me the gift of renewed life and purpose.

TRIBUTE

...how I do long for a full expression of everything that is in me, a free outpouring of everything I feel. I have patience, I have love of men and women and children and trees - I can watch over a thing for years - in fact forever and nurse it into its full strength, but there is still a part of me that yearns for the unknown perfection-not a religious, heavenly perfection but a full-bodied earthly perfection that is fragile as all life and as sweet.

William Carlos Williams MD
1916 letter to his mother

Contents

PHOTOGRAPHS

CHAPTER 1
A SUMMER AFTERNOON

It was late August 1939, a time filled with turmoil and anxiety in Europe as Hitler moved toward further invasions, events much too far removed from this ten year old driven mostly by the day's baseball scores. It was just another wind-down long hot summer day for this city kid from uptown Washington Heights in Manhattan. The days and weeks had stretched out endlessly that summer. The boring, inevitable grind toward school re-opening seemed to move at a snail's pace.

That summer I watched sadly as my mother became increasingly debilitated by the pain of her cancer. I was old enough to appreciate just how much this illness had set her apart from the rest of us in the family.

It seemed that my mother had been ill for most of my ten years, although I did have some recollection of her soft, wavy, blond hair, her dimpled cheeks and broad smile, all before her troubles began. It was different now. I could sense how easily she tired, how quickly she was out of breath, even with the least exertion. Climbing the stairs to our apartment on the third floor had become a challenge that required all of her strength. Several times that summer I had glimpsed her obvious exhaustion, her ashen face, as she entered our apartment after having to grip the handrail and pull herself up the long way from the street level.

That afternoon we were finishing lunch. I was totally

13

bored and my mother took pity on me. "I'm going to the store," she said, and asked if I wanted to join her, just to have something to do. While she went into the bedroom for her hat I thought about it, finally deciding, that instead, I would not go to the store but would wait to help her with the groceries when she returned. Naturally, I didn't say anything about it to her.

I remember hanging around the front of the apartment house after she'd gone. Some of my buddies appeared and asked if I wanted to join in a softball game in our P.S. 189 schoolyard, located just around the corner. Two of the best hitters in the group chose up sides, and included me on one of the teams. This put me in a quandary. After a moment's hesitation I declined, but made a compromise to cover my afternoon's mission.

"Oh, it's too hot, but I'll go over to the school," I said. Of course, I couldn't let them know I was waiting for my mother.

I decided to take up a good vantage point at the entrance to the play area so that I could easily spot my mother when she returned. My head was constantly moving left and right between the baseball field and our building entrance across the street. It became more like watching tennis than baseball.

The afternoon wore on. The play was indifferent, as usual. Neither side was doing anything spectacular. It was an ordinary softball game on a hot summer's day. There were few hits and too many embarrassing errors. Once in a while there was a particularly good catch or fielding effort. An occasional booming hit kept the interest alive. Whatever the action, I continued to make a concerted effort to focus my attention on where I expected to see my mother.

14

1

The game started to wind down. We were all becoming bored and the heat had, by now, consumed everyone's energy and interest. As the teams began to disperse I had a troubled sense that it was very late. My mother should have been home by now. I had been watching carefully. My whole plan had been to help the moment I saw her. Yet she had not appeared.

Waving to my friends, I ran across the street and up the two flights of stairs to our apartment. I gasped and had an awful, sinking feeling. The front door was not quite closed. I could not believe it. My mother was home. I had failed her completely. Consumed with a sickening, guilt-ridden, choked-up feeling, I slowed at the threshold and opened the door softly.

There sat my mother on a kitchen stool. Uncomfortable. Out of breath. So pale. Two large grocery bags sat on a table nearby like monstrous statues renouncing me as both thoughtless and uncaring. My mother found the strength and showed the sensitivity to greet me with a smile and inquire about my afternoon.

"Mom, I'm so sorry I missed you. I was trying to watch for you from the schoolyard to help with the groceries. I feel badly you had to carry them yourself."

"It's all right," she replied with emphasis in her voice trying to console me. "The thought is what really matters. I know how much you try to help. You're always such a comfort to me," she said.

On September 1, 1939, my mother died at age 39. On that same day Germany invaded Austria and World War II began.

17

CHAPTER 2
EMERGING IDENTITY

My father quickly decided to vacate our apartment on Washington Heights and so moved my older sister, Irene, and me downtown to his dental office suite on Central Park West. This set the stage for intense problems in adjustment, frequent G.I. and other somatic complaints, and years of transient living. We slept on day beds in the two waiting rooms; a small kitchenette made do for meals. I sequestered myself in the confines of a large closet or a bathroom where I did my homework and had some privacy from waiting patients. The sudden, wrenching loss of my friends and all that I knew in Washington Heights left me bewildered, and this emptiness could not be repaired by visits to the old neighborhood on weekends. In time, I settled into a routine at P.S. 87, the local elementary school. Not wishing to attend the trade high school that was available in my school district, I was able to use my Aunt Henny's uptown address to register at George Washington High School a short distance from where we used to live and commuted by subway.

Intense and compulsive in high school, I became the leader of Arista, the academic honor society and Captain of the Honor Ushers Corps. I graduated valedictorian with many awards. My applications to both Harvard and Yale were rejected, however, and so I went on to an indifferent record as a pre-med day student at Columbia College. My

19

goal then, and as far back as I could remember, was medical school, yet I had not one acceptance note on graduation. I decided to re-apply and, at the suggestion of a friend, completed a master's degree in public health education in one year at the Columbia University School of Public Health.

After this course of study was completed, I applied again to med school and again was rejected. Trained now as a health educator, I resigned myself to being yet another addition to the heap of med school rejects. A feeling of failure enveloped me, a feeling similar to the one I had experienced that summer afternoon when I had been unable to help my mother.

While I was on a summer public health fieldwork training with the City Health Department in Charlotte, North Carolina in 1950, my father died suddenly. We had not been close in his final years. I had increasingly rejected his sloppy professionalism, his superficial socializing with the well-to-do, and his compulsive gambling. It was a sad and ironic close to his life that he had died of a heart attack on a taxi ride home from the racetrack. I thought about what our lives as a family had become in the eleven years since the death of my mother, and how little happiness he had experienced in those years. Totally on my own now, I was unaware that my flight home from Charlotte would be the first of many to come.

Searching for my next move, I decided to attend a National Tuberculosis and Health Association (NTA) training course in Wisconsin. Following visits to possible job sites in Iowa and Nebraska and without much enthusiasm, I accepted an entry-level position at the Passaic County (NJ) TB and Health Association in Patterson. I was motivated, in part, to accept this job as it would enable me to take more education courses at Teachers' College - courses that had interested me while in public health graduate school. Also my new office location would be near Aunt Chub and Uncle Abe and I could now easily visit my sister Irene and her family in Long Island. In retrospect. the only outstanding experiences I can remember of that year in Patterson were the contacts I made and maintained with the multi-racial Ramapo Mountain Indians still living in Ringwood amidst the old iron mines of northern Passaic County, a settlement that had been active in Revolutionary times. A high rate of tuberculosis in this group became the focus of my health education efforts.

By age twenty-two, I found myself floundering in a job with no future, uncertain about what to do next, still plagued by that persistent sense of failure. The Korean War was on. My draft board notified me that I was eligible for call-up. At the pre-induction screening on Governor's Island, my attitude was one of complete indifference. It was as if I were an outsider looking disconnectedly at some other person's future. I was totally resigned to let fate take its course, willingly allowing myself to be swept along by whatever was in store for me as a draftee.

Someone told me about eligibility as an officer in the army medical administration corps. I found this intriguing enough to proceed with the preliminary screening exam, but never followed through. Eventually, I heard about another option of becoming an officer of the U.S. Public Health Service – a branch of the armed forces in wartime with Navy equivalent ranks. The possibility of this alternative somehow pulled me out of my pervasive haze of malaise and indifference that defined that period in my life.

While I had certainly become familiar with the Public Health Service in graduate school and knew something about its activities with the states and Indian Health Service, I was unaware of the extensive international programs with which it was involved. During an

21

exploratory visit to Washington, D.C. at this time, I learned about its technical assistance to countries in Europe under the Marshall Plan, and to other parts of the world through the Point Four Program. I was offered an international assignment to one of these programs and readily accepted.

I found myself now in a heated race with my draft board. I really wanted that PHS commission, wherever in the world it would take me. Of course, there were the usual delays. Programs in the field had to be notified about my existence and availability. Who would want to take a twenty-two year old health educator only a year out of public health school and with very limited experience? Washington shopped around for me. Greece rejected me after some consideration. Vietnam was being explored as a strong possibility. Whatever the destination, I realized that I was about to be drafted unless I had a Public Health Service commission. I was constantly on the phone with Washington to remind them of my plight. I quit my job at the tuberculosis and health association and stayed with my sister in Long Island to prepare for whatever would be in store for me.

I received my notice to appear for induction into the army. It was coming down to the wire. Washington had not been able to obtain a definite overseas commitment for me. I had gone from this initial attitude of not caring what would happen to me, to one of determination to somehow become a PHS officer. My goal-driven personality must have connected my recent training with a possible future PHS career. Perhaps it was all about the romance of overseas service for someone who had no ties or connections. Without question, I would lose this possibility unless something happened quickly. Finally, a telegraphed commission by the Public Health Service saved the day. I was ordered for temporary duty to Washington without a definite assignment!

22

***

Washington, D.C. in the smoldering heat of the summer of 1951. Not much air-conditioning but lots of time to hang out while an assignment was being drawn up for me. There was still a possibility of being assigned to Vietnam. I obtained permission to attend the Vietnamese language program every morning at the State Department Foreign Language Institute.

I remember Congress being in session at the time. I became one of the afternoon regulars in the House gallery, inwardly cheering on the stalwarts of foreign aid, while damning the budget cutters. Of course, the air-conditioned atmosphere helped to while away the sweltering hours as I anxiously awaited my fate.

Fall approached. I continued my Vietnamese studies but still was given no overseas assignment. The congressional debates began to pale. I was becoming yet another young government employee on the Washington scene with a budding social life, with an expanding array of the many things to do and see there, and yet, at all times, with a fading awareness that it was all temporary. I had discovered Wesley Hall, an uptown singles residence with a dorm-like atmosphere, good food service, and plenty of social contacts. The move to this residence greatly mitigated the feeling of anonymity associated with living and working in the Capitol, and provided a strongly positive lifestyle in contrast to what I had left behind.

This casual and now comfortable routine came to an abrupt end with the announcement that I would be going to Burma. *(And this just when I was becoming proficient with "good morning" in Vietnamese!)* I had to scramble to the atlas for orientation. Since I was to leave within a matter of weeks, it would not be possible to re-start a

23

language program. There was some comfort in the thought that my language training efforts might have general benefits at a later time. As it turned out, specific orientation to the Burmese assignment was left up to me entirely and consisted in my becoming familiar with limited library references. However, in preparation and for some additional technical background, I did manage a few days of observing public health sanitation activities in rural Georgia.

After almost five months of a carefree Washington life style, I looked forward to this next phase in my life. I had no pre-conceived ideas. It seemed entirely natural for me to move on. I thought little about the two-year time commitment, or that this constituted Korean War service. I hadn't followed events of the conflict with any regularity. Although I had limited previous professional experience and no overseas travel experience, I relished the trip ahead as an adventure in itself.

Propeller-powered air travel in 1951 was more relaxed and adventurous than by today's standards. A full three days from New York to Burma, including overnight from New York to Los Angeles. A full day to Honolulu. A flight through the night to Hong Kong and then onto Rangoon the next day. The gradual transition through the time zones into this totally different world left me with no doubts, no concerns, ready to soak this new experience up like a very dry sponge.

Descending from the airplane to the Rangoon tarmac that November day in 1951, the first thing that struck me was the different quality of the air. It was a heat I had never experienced before. The mingling of vegetation and pungent odors in the air sharpened my senses. I would quickly adjust to this background, yet never really lose my awareness of it. Several senior Public Health Service officers who had been on the plane with me were greeted effusively. Being the new man, I came forward, introduced

24

myself, and took my place to the rear of the group. Rank made a difference.

No matter, I was finally on the ground in Burma. My world would never be the same.

CHAPTER 3
BURMESE DAYS

When I arrived in Burma (now Myanmar), I found the country in an unsettled, unstable political state. In 1951, Burma was just three years out from having gained independence from British colonial rule. This was also at a time shortly after the assassination of its first leader, General Aung San. Moreover, the Shan States to the north and east were attempting to achieve their own autonomous political status and an active insurrection was heating up. It was both an exciting and uncertain time of transition.

In order to become better acquainted with its public health education needs, I quickly learned that Burma was a predominantly rural country. There was rice growing in the central low lands, fishing in southern and western deltas, and poppy growing in the northern hills adjacent to China. Everywhere golden pagodas dotted the green fields. In some areas like Pagan, pagodas were the predominant "crop". Water buffalo provided much of the transportation as well as much of the cultivation of the fields, often clogging the narrow roads.

The gentle, quiet Burmese people were enmeshed in this tranquil rural scene. They were a people languid and soft-spoken. Their always colorful wrap-around skirt (longyi), worn by both sexes, was topped off for women by a lacy blouse, while the men were often bare from the waist up. To this day the longyi is my pajama of choice.

Rangoon, the capital (now Yangon) reflected its

location as a port on the Irrawardy River, with a polyglot population of Indian and Chinese merchants, European firms, and streets crowded with stalls, roving sellers of pots and pans, barbers, dentists, ear cleaners. A mixture of civilian and old military vehicles jammed the roads, sharing the narrow right-of-way with ancient, overcrowded buses, bullocks, horses, and the occasional goat, not to mention roving bands of beggar children. Standing on any street corner in downtown Rangoon provided a panorama of passing humanity of every shape, size, and color.

Mandalay, to the north, had a much slower pace, the horse competing with the car as the means of transportation. The old colonial style layout of English-named streets and traffic 'roundabouts contrasted with run-down bungalows, unused tennis courts, forming a pervading air of days gone-by. A much more apparent Chinese merchant population conducted business, while Burmese street stalls seemed to have cropped up only in recent times, crowding out run-down buildings and unused storefronts.

Religion lay at the core of the people's daily life: for the Burmese it was Buddhism along with a smattering of Christianity; for the Indian population it was Hinduism and Islam. The Chinese remained a separate and uncertain group.

Weather in Burma was not to be taken lightly. The three seasons of hot, wet, and dry contrasted one another sharply. Cool temperatures during the dry period gave way to the very hot season, and the hot periods were relieved by the northwest monsoon. The rains could be continuous for days at a time, literally soaking everything and causing mildew indoors. Downpours of over fifteen inches of rain a day were not unusual in the western Arakan (Bengal) delta area, where the sound of rain on a tin roof could be deafening. No wonder major religious festivals coincided

3A

with changes in the weather, such as the water festival at Buddhist New Year at the end of the dry season, the Indian Dewali, and the Muslim Id holidays.

American culture, technology, and expectations descended into this milieu in the form of the United States Special Technical and Economic Mission to Burma (S.T.E.M.). An outgrowth of President Truman's Point Four Program to offer technical and economic assistance to emerging Asian nations in need, STEM aimed to provide help in many fields and train local personnel. The Public Health Service staffed the health component. This included career officers and draftees like myself since the PHS is a branch of the armed forces (navy equivalent) in wartime. While the American Embassy in Rangoon served as our administrative headquarters, we generally worked in the Health Ministry offices located in various other parts of the city. We rarely came downtown. The Marine guards posted at the embassy entrance served as a reminder to the colorful multitudes passing by that Uncle Sam was ever watchful of us.

At the time, health conditions in Burma reflected a relatively small population with adequate food and water resources and with only limited infectious disease. Malaria was of chief concern, especially in the low-lying delta areas. Environmental sanitation improvements constituted the greatest needs ranging from improving water resources quality, to waste removal, to general cleanliness. Enhancing diet and nutrition were also high on the list. My field of health education was at the root of both the public health problems and their solutions.

By the time I arrived, a health education program had already been set up by my senior counterpart located in a demonstration health center on the outskirts of Rangoon. This provided me with a good orientation to the country monitoring the work already in progress. Expansion to a national program had begun to emerge when, some

31

months after my arrival, my colleague became ill and left for treatment. With this occurrence, the development of the Bureau of Health Education, Burma Department of Health and Medical Services, then became my responsibility at the age of twenty-four.

Directly behind my ground floor office window at the Bureau, an ancient cemetery was in full frame. This served as a visual reminder to me, to all of us in the department, to re-double our efforts in improving health and delaying the inevitable. In a matter of months, I had a staff of two senior public health inspectors - my counterparts in training to be health educators, along with an artist and a media specialist, and the inevitable head clerk. With my counterparts, I began extensive travel to unrestricted parts of the country. This included the Northern Shan States in the Golden Triangle with China; due north to the hill country and Mandalay; to Lashio and the beginning of the old World War II Burma Road; and to the western delta at Akyab. We worked with the STEM team in each area to demonstrate community organization techniques with local health stations and to incorporate health education materials - posters, leaflets, and exhibits - into their programs. Audio-visual equipment was always in demand. Viewing films or slides was often a totally new experience for the villagers we visited on these trips.

Back at the Bureau office, I also functioned as an administrator and bureaucrat. Just keeping the office running with stationery and paper clips took a certain amount of ingenuity. Assuring monthly payment for my staff required subtle, stealthy visits to a relative of a relative in the Ministry of Finance.

Our audio-visual equipment was jealously guarded in the home of the director of public health. A complicated inter-personal strategy to obtain a projector for use on a field visit included arranging an appointment with the director's wife who kept the closet keys on her person.

3B

Only after assurance about the exact location and purpose of the request would the equipment be made available, provided the Director approved. The entire process required a certain amount of social skill and finesse.

I also functioned as Education Office of the STEM mission – a privilege given to the low man on the totem pole. It involved coordinating travel arrangements for Burmese selected by the various programs for further training in the United States. I informed the twenty-five trainees in the first group about passport requirements and essentials of confirmed air travel. In each case I was assured that arrangements had been made. A grand send-off at the Rangoon airport attended by the Health Minister was followed the next day by a cable from London indicating the entire group had arrived with no confirmed reservations onward to the United States. Ultimately, after much negotiation, a special charter flight had to be arranged to accommodate the group at the height of the travel season. To my dismay, I later learned that a trainee's relative had opened up a "travel office" adjacent to the embassy, and simply processed tickets only as far as London. Summoned to the Ambassador's office soon after, and in the presence of the Mission Director, I was strongly reprimanded and had considerable difficulty facing my colleagues.

Apart from work at the mission, life for me in Burma was interesting and varied. Living in the lap of luxury at the Strand Hotel just around the corner from the American Embassy during my first days in Burma didn't quite suit me. I soon moved away from downtown to a flat in "Golden Valley" near the Shwedagon Pagoda, sharing a big old house with two other PHS officers. I had my own Jeep and driver for official use, with access to the vehicle whenever needed. I often went to the Shwedagon to observe and learn about Buddhism and meditation. A massive golden spire surrounded by walkways and open

35

areas with many satellite pagodas, the Shwedagon is by far the largest in Burma, and a focus for the entire Rangoon area. And it was an easy walk from my digs.

I developed close friendships with a number of Burmese, visited their homes often and participated with them in festivals and holidays. Contacts were fairly close with the STEM Mission health staff, but very limited with embassy personnel. Perhaps this constituted my reverse snobbery - a reaction to my feeling that many in the embassy showed little interest in the country or its people.

Apart from fairly extensive travel around Burma, I also took some time off to visit Ceylon (now Sri Lanka), and virtually circumnavigated India by train and plane. I also toured Bangkok and nearby Thailand areas. With my Burma experience background, these travels helped to greatly expand my knowledge and understanding of the entire Southeast Asian region.

Toward the end of my two-year period, the international political situation changed greatly. A truce had been declared in Korea and the new Eisenhower administration added *military* assistance to the scope of aid missions such as ours in Burma. While continuing to provide technical and economic assistance to the country, the United States had begun military assistance to the Nationalist Chinese at the Burma/Thai/Chinese border. Within weeks of this information being made public the Burmese Government terminated the U. S. Aid Agreement and we were forced to leave abruptly. Some thought that the *Armed Forces of the United States* ID card each of us carried may have been incriminating at this juncture and added to the disruption. Burma quickly changed to a military dictatorship in an attempt to isolate itself from its powerful Indian and Chinese neighbors, with resultant social, economic, and political decline for years to come.

I had mixed feelings about going home. I truly loved my experience in Burma – its people, countryside, and its gentle way of life. But being a health educator with a master's degree still provided little personal satisfaction for me. I did not have the sense of being a true professional. Medical school was still on my mind even though it seemed totally out of reach. Casting about for what to do, I contacted Professor Herbert Walker at Teacher's College, Columbia University, whom I had known from my days at graduate school. He encouraged me to return and complete a Doctor of Education program as his Graduate Assistant. At the time this seemed to be a logical next move.

The departure from Rangoon in September 1953 was tearful; the parties and receptions long remembered. I often attended in full Burmese dress with the traditional hat (gombong), jacket, and skirt (longyi). A deep feeling of family bound me, especially to my colleagues at the Health Education Bureau with whom I had worked so closely, and to others at the Health Ministry. There were no comparable relationships between myself and either STEM or embassy staff.

The return trip westward briefly prolonged my Burmese contacts. I accidentally met my counterpart in Rome who had been in the States for training. It was a wonderful reminder that the work would continue after I left and hopefully become a permanent part of the Burmese landscape. This dream was realized during a return visit to Rangoon (now Yangon) in 2003 with my daughter Martha. Quite by chance we met the then Director of the Health Education Bureau who enthusiastically assured us that the work started almost six decades previously had indeed continued and greatly expanded. It was a happy revelation.

CHAPTER 4
TEARDROP of INDIA

Obstructing the traffic flow by casually attempting to board a New York City bus during rush hour, I made my way uptown to Columbia University. The route had always been well known to me, yet after two years in Burma, I felt like a first-time tourist, marveling at the tall buildings and congested streets. To my chagrin, accommodation in the Columbia graduate dorm was unavailable, and I was forced to grudgingly accept a place at Whittier Hall for Teachers College students located north of the main Columbia campus center.

Co-ed dormitory life in those days meant alternating male and female floors with strict enforcement of the rules, but it also turned out to be an excellent place for an expatriate like myself to develop some much needed friendships. It was here that I met Barbara Boyd, a nursing education student and a dormitory co-resident, later to become my wife.

Whittier was my base for the next fourteen months of intense activity centered on the task of completing a Doctor of Education degree. I literally holed up in a quiet office provided by Professor Herbert Walker, my major advisor in health education. Professor Walker helped guide me through the rigors of needed course work and the inevitable dissertation. In a short time, we developed a very close relationship, one that would expand to include

39

his wife, Vivian. In time, the Walkers would become god-parents of Lisa, our first child.

I had never clearly articulated to myself a rationale for returning to Columbia and pursuing a doctorate. I was simply trying things out, experimenting, seeing where they might take me, filling in the void of not becoming a real doctor. With no clear goal in mind, I used my international technical aid experience, with Burma as an example, for my dissertation entitled *Health Education in Public Health Programs for Underdeveloped Areas*. My varied interests were reflected in the dissertation committee consisting of, in addition to Dr. Walker, professors of public health, and international education.

Somehow this goal was finalized within a year - a time that allowed for some socializing with Barbara and the TC gang in the spring and with frequent summer trips to Jones Beach on Long Island. At the beach, soaking up the sun to counteract our long winter indoors, I always made it a point of showing off my Burmese "credentials" by demonstrating the proper way to tie my longyi .

Herb Walker was keen on getting me placed in a teaching position in health education at Cortland State Teachers College in Upstate New York. I had no real interest in doing this but still went for the interview out of courtesy. The position was offered to me, yet I saw nothing but a dead end ahead. Obviously, I wasn't ready to settle down. More international experience was on my mind.

I contacted the World Health Organization (WHO), and accepted a two-year assignment as Health Education Adviser to Ceylon. Dr. Walker, always the gentleman, smiled and offered his best wishes.

By then, Barbara and I were in a serious relationship. I left for my assignment in Ceylon with both of us very much unsettled as to our future plans. During a briefing at WHO headquarters in Geneva, I sought the advice of an

4A

attorney about our getting married. Shortly after arriving in Colombo, I then cabled my proposal to Barbara. Strong opposition from her parents weighed heavily in her decision not to join me then, but we agreed that this could change when I returned to the States. In retrospect, my reaction reflected several emotions. One was in understanding Barbara's situation in having been raised by devout Catholic parents who had had very little experience beyond their restricted parochial lives, but there was another feeling as well - a twinge of my own doubt about going forward with marriage.

When I arrived in Colombo in the fall of 1954, it felt as if I were returning to Southeast Asia as home after an extended, whirlwind leave. Ceylon (now Sri Lanka) was very different from Burma. It had been culturally battered by successive exposures to Portuguese, Dutch, and finally, British invaders. Intermarriage and remnants of colonial rule had greatly altered the Sinhalese people and culture. Moreover, importation of Tamil laborers from south India to work the tea plantations had added a northern minority population. This group would, years after my period of service in the country, unsuccessfully spend two decades fighting a bloody civil war of independence on the island. In this small island country some 300 miles long and 100 miles wide, I felt the people were less serene and more complicated than the Burmese. In geographical perspective, Ceylon seemed like a teardrop of India.

Tea was king in the central hills and valleys, while subsistence agriculture and fishing predominated along the coasts. Having a standard of living well above that of other Southeast Asian countries, Ceylon also had a very high level of literacy, good quality of roads and communication, with a unique lifestyle all its own.

Colombo, located on the central western coast on the Indian Ocean, was a cosmopolitan city and a major port. A bustling downtown business area had considerable

43

sophistication balanced by a large open bazaar. Traffic consisted of every type of vehicle, and, on occasion, the work-elephant would appear from the countryside with the handler in charge, hauling a large piece of timber or pulling a container of building material.

Important ancient historical and religious sites at Kandy in the foothills, Polonnaruwa and Anuradhapura on the western coast, were among many well-preserved areas where one could get a glimpse of a proud heritage that predated, by far, the influence of foreign invaders. Eastern towns of Trincomalee and Batticaloa had remnants of British naval activity; Jaffna in the extreme north encompassed the Tamil separatist population and was poles apart from the Sinhalese fishing villages around Hambantota and Galle in the extreme south. Nuwara Eliya, the jewel at the peak of the highest hills (6000 feet) amidst the finest tea plantations, was a hill station famed for its panoramic views of the tea fields, delightfully cool climate, and guest houses offering every European convenience. Topography, like everything else in Ceylon, reflected the blending influences of peoples and cultures that had come into contact with the island over the years.

Everywhere I could feel the mixing of traditional culture with European contact. A memorable example was the common practice among elderly Sinhalese men of sewing pant legs to the bottom of the traditional longyi or sarong. In this fashion, they were able to bridge the cultural divide by melding the old and new with this ingenious compromise, walking in trousers and the traditional dress as one garment.

English was spoken widely, even in Singhalese villages, although less so in the Tamil area in the north. English language newspapers were quite popular. Yet this Western influence appeared, at times, to be superficial. A case in point was on the occasion of an eclipse of the sun during which time Ceylon offered the most optimum

4B

scientific world view for the occasion. Scientists from around the world set up their equipment. The English language media offered daily technical reports about the upcoming phenomena. The day after the eclipse had occurred people from every social and economic level, including religious leaders, professionals, and politicians, reported to hospitals and dispensaries with severe gastrointestinal symptoms. Epidemiologic investigation soon confirmed widespread ingestion by the populace of a potion taken just as the moon crossed the sun - an elixir that had been recommended in the Sinhalese press. A sort of national embarrassment about this incident was lampooned for quite a long time afterwards in all the media.

I had a certain sensitivity to this cultural mixture in Ceylon, especially the deep intrusion and disruption of Western influence. This followed from my close identification and recent experience with the "simpler" and perhaps "purer" Burmese lifestyle - a way of life that seemed, in retrospect, more straightforward. On the one hand, Ceylon appeared to have many elements of sophistication stemming from Western influences. Yet, like the eclipse incident, this often proved to be superficial, and would sometimes complicate interpersonal communication and relationships.

What was I doing on a two-year assignment in Ceylon, anyway? Having quickly completed my Ed.D., the prospect of settling down to a state-side teaching job had held little appeal, and an offer from WHO couldn't be refused. At the time, I was still giving little serious thought about my future, including no further thought about medical school. My instructions at WHO headquarters in Geneva, Switzerland were to help develop a national health education program. Unlike the rudimentary beginnings in Burma, the assignment to Ceylon started off on much more direct and organized level.

I shared an office with the two top-level medical administrators of the Ceylon Health and Medical Services in Colombo. The old British bureaucracy had been retained in the system... and then some. All business was strictly conducted by communicating through huge numbers of laced subject files brought to each desk by the ever-present peon, a person who stood by or waited outside for instructions. Work progressed from the "in" to "out" piles on each desk, the latter files being dispersed to some mysterious central location where files would all be redistributed. A day would progress by movement from the two piles, with little, if any, conversation between the room occupants. Some excitement might follow receipt of a file marked "urgent", and the peon would wait and swing into action after the proper entry was made. Other more serious tags included "immediate", and "most immediate", with the commensurate animation by both director and peon. Both assistant directors at the time were Burghers (of Dutch ancestry) and took the whole system very seriously. I tried to maintain a sense of humor, communicate as best I could, and attempt to get out into the field whenever possible.

The task for me was straightforward: examine the existing structure and organization of the Health Department, and set up a national system for health education services that would operate at the local level. In the atmosphere of that second floor white-washed room overlooking the Indian Ocean with my two assistant director colleagues, the peon, and the files, I prepared *Health Education in Ceylon: A Report with Recommendations*, published by the Ceylon Government Press. Like any blueprint, I followed the plan to the letter. Existing local health units were selected strategically as regional centers along with a group of well-experienced Public Health Inspectors recruited for health education training. Back at the office, I developed curriculum for a three-month course given at Kalutera, a demonstration health center south of Colombo where the inspectors were in residence. I did most of the teaching, supplemented by lectures and demonstrations from specialists in media, psychology, teaching, and other fields from the University of Ceylon. During this period the students and I got to know each other well.

My follow-up field visits were crucial in helping the staff get started. I literally toured every part of Ceylon, covering 25,000 miles in a year. A wonderful experience, as well, to be guided by my students through local tea factories, historical sites, port facilities, and conservation areas. It was an opportunity not available to the casual visitor to the island. After my director-counterpart was appointed, these visits added an assurance to future growth of the work that had been started, and enabled me to minimize time spent amidst the files and desks in Colombo.

Occasional visits to WHO regional headquarters in New Delhi also helped change the pace and gave me a perspective on related public health developments in the entire Southeast Asia area. A major vacation trip took me briefly back to Rangoon by ship, revisiting old haunts with my former Burmese colleagues. The vacation included a trip by air to Saigon (now Ho Chi Min City), Vietnam (then French but becoming politically restless), where I visited a Teachers College classmate whom I had encouraged to take a foreign assignment. He loved the work and helped me to experience the area.

Then I traveled on to Japan on a French passenger vessel. Virtually no English was spoken. Playing competitive bridge games aboard ship in French and touring Japan with a Japanese/French translator were both major challenges that turned out to be instructive and enjoyable.

Future WHO assignments were offered to me toward

49

the completion of these two busy years. Indonesia would be next, but I did not consider this seriously. At the time all this good work accomplished in Ceylon did not register as important enough for a career in international health education. Yet, as I later discovered, my years in Ceylon had set down the basis for what has become the current Health Education Bureau within the Ministry of Health - with programs at all levels of government and extensive training of staff, including graduate education. Truly a legacy for which I am exceedingly proud!

However, I again decided to return to the States, this time for a doctoral program in medical sociology on a Commonwealth Fund Fellowship at Yale - back to the familiar halls of ivy and another period of stateside readjustment. Strangely, this regular change of direction neither seemed unusual nor did it trouble me in any way. I considered it all part of my continuing process in gathering more experience and training in a quest to find myself.

CHAPTER 5
SOUTH PACIFIC INTERLUDE

The eleven month period following my return to the States from Ceylon was a productive one, busy with earning a Master's Degree and working on a Ph.D. in (Medical) Sociology at Yale. Barbara and I renewed our relationship, hesitatingly at first, but gradually the flame re-ignited with weekends spent either in New Haven or in New York. We again spoke seriously of marriage against this background of how best to deal with our religious differences. It was difficult for Barbara who had been given a strong Catholic training and who, in high school, had even received a prize in religion! A compromise was found thanks to a very liberal Columbia Catholic Chaplain who neither required me to convert nor mandated our children be baptized into the faith.

Quite by accident, our honeymoon site ended up being a quaint cabin on Lake George. This cabin would serve as our home during June 1957 while we prepared for my next WHO assignment as Health Education Advisor to the South Pacific Commission. Once again an offer from WHO had put into motion what was becoming my zigzag pattern of alternating academia with overseas service. This assignment, however, now included a willing partner equally enthusiastic about travel, and one who also happened to be a nurse with a public health background. Taking a leave from the Yale Fellowship in July 1957, we set out for Noumea, New Caledonia, a thousand miles east of Sydney, Australia.

The booking agent at Cook's Travel in New York did not have a clue about how to reach our destination and somewhat painfully referred to a world map in order to identify pertinent travel points along the way. With the itinerary finalized, we traveled from Los Angeles in the propeller plane of that era, a trip which included reclining comfort and beautifully prepared meals. It was an unhurried affair. First, a ten hour flight to Hawaii with an overnight stop in Honolulu. Then, a journey westward through the eastern Pacific with a middle-of-the-night deplaning for hand-pumped refueling on Johnson Island, landing in Fiji the next day. Next, onto Auckland, New Zealand with the final leg to Noumea, New Caledonia. Three days and many time zones later, we arrived on the island, dazed by the travel experience yet fascinated by the mix of New Orleans style architecture, French cuisine, and Melanesian culture.

We soon learned that New Caledonia had been a French penal colony at the turn of the 20th century. A western Melanesian island in the spectacular blue/green Coral Sea, it had untouched golden sand beaches whose waters were often inhabited by sea creatures that could be poisonous, compelling caution when swimming. Mountainous, with extensive nickel deposits for world export, the island was little developed other than the western town of Noumea and hamlets scattered to the north. The few roads on the island had been paved with a nickel mixture that would literally sand down a tire's tread, requiring a tire check after each hour-long airport trip.

Noumea felt like a sleepy provincial French town of the late 19th century with its shuttered wood houses, filigree appointments, and narrow streets. Traffic was sparse, cars mostly of French make, along with a few

52

horse-drawn vehicles. The climate was an eternal spring with little variation throughout the year. On arrival in July, we headed for the gleaming beach daily. Virtually empty, we wondered at the seeming indifference of residents to this gift of nature and soon learned that the low temperatures at this time of year, about five degrees below summer readings, were prohibitive to the acclimated. By the same time the following year, we, too, felt this temperature difference, and avoided the beaches like everyone else.

Unlike the period clapboard filigreed residential structures in the center of town, we lived in an upstairs apartment in a modern stucco house on Mt. Coffin, a hilly area overlooking the Coral Sea. While the view provided a visual delight, there was a constant throttling noise outside our windows from motorcycle engines as they prepared to climb the hill. I might have been the only resident ever to have slept each night in that gorgeous location using earplugs.

The population of the town reflected three distinct ethnic groups. The native Melanesians of dark color were akin to the large indigenous populations of the western Pacific islands. Mostly farmers, their numbers were small in the towns where they were usually employed in service activities or maintained small shops. Members of the second ethnic group were descendants of the original penal colony settlers. They appeared to be Caucasian and were bilingual with French and English. Finally, there were the French functionaries themselves who were much in evidence, often in uniform, working in administrative, security, and other government roles. Detachments of the French Foreign Legion remained a constant presence as well. Other European nationals conducted business while Chinese merchants were everywhere. Americans were few: Bob Shackleton, the U.S. Counsel for the Pacific, and his wife Gilberte, would become life-long friends; Ben, the local butcher, a World War II navy veteran and native Rhode Islander, had returned to the island after the war to settle down in Noumea.

The South Pacific Commission was a multinational group. Founded after World War II by Australia, France, Great Britain, Netherlands, New Zealand, and the USA to address social, economic, and health concerns of dependent South Pacific island territories, the Commission was located in Noumea at the former World War II headquarters of the US 7th fleet. In addition to the administrative staff (an American served as Secretary-General at the time), specialists in various fields carried out the programs established at the periodic meetings of the Commission. The fascinating eighteenth and nineteenth century history of Western acquisition of South Pacific islands, including the pre-World War I German territories under League of Nations mandates to Australia, the Netherlands, and New Zealand, continued to play out in the manipulations of these representative Commission governments. In time, I developed a strong conviction that the developmental activity efforts were merely a thin veneer covering the true aim of these countries to eventually divest themselves of these far-away places.

My function in Noumea was to participate in a health education training course for South Pacific health workers - workers who ranged in backgrounds from an Australian aboriginal having little formal education to a French-speaking Polynesian with a baccalaureate degree. The concept of the course originated with a senior colleague at the WHO Regional Office in Manila. He prevailed on the South Pacific Commission for use of its facilities in Noumea where lectures and demonstrations would be given. He did the initial organizational work in conjunction with the Commission medical director, a delightful, charming French physician who had long previous experience with the French Colonial Medical

5A

Service and the Foreign Legion. I served a faculty role and, at the completion of the course, had the enviable assignment of traveling the South Pacific to follow up with the students - a very diverse group of islanders who had been selected prior to our arrival.

The *dramatis personae* included a colorful, congenial group of students from American Samoa, Australia, Australian New Guinea (now Papua/New Guinea), British Solomon Islands Protectorate (new independent Solomon Islands), British Cook Islands (now independent), Dutch New Guinea (now Indonesian Irian Jaya), British Fiji (now independent), British/French New Hebrides Condominium (now Vanuatu), French Tahiti, and Western Samoa (a New Zealand protectorate, now independent). Curiously, there was no representation from New Caledonia itself. All members spoke English but again education and socio-cultural backgrounds varied greatly. For most of the people in this group it was a once in a lifetime travel opportunity, a first experience in flying for many, and a chance to experience life on another island.

In conversations getting to know the students, we were often asked, "How big is your island?" After all, didn't everyone live on some kind of an island?

An Australian educator and his assistant had the responsibility for the course procedures. A New Zealand specialist in education from the Commission staff also participated in the pedagogical approach. The Commission medical director and assistant medical director (Scottish), had a peripheral involvement in the medical course content. At the head of this operation stood my senior American colleague, the WHO regional health education adviser from Manila.

National pride and strong personality differences among these players resulted in the daily conflicts, disagreements, and differences of opinion about course management that resulted in concerns affecting all of us.

A major issue centered on course procedure. Daily sessions initially consisted of stiff, formal lectures that the students expected and to which the Australian staff were accustomed. In spite of much gnashing of teeth and overt opposition by some of the professionals, I was able to help direct the course toward one involving more student interaction and group participation - not easy in a situation with such diverse cultural and educational backgrounds. In the end, though, it was rewarding when it became clear that everyone had something to contribute and that we could learn a great deal from each other – not just from the lecturer. This kind of interaction also spilled over into improving communication and social contacts among the students housed in Commission facilities.

At the conclusion of the course, my follow-up travel took center stage. The two-fold purpose involved helping each trainee to identify ways of integrating health education into his or her activities as well as recommending to governments how the work could be more broadly implemented. In many ways, with the whole Pacific to cover, west to east, a propeller airplane above, and lots of water below, this became a challenging assignment.

I prepared myself for this work by intensely studying the history and geography of each area I would be visiting using the extensive Commission library. It was fascinating to learn that pre-World War I Germany had actively colonized much of the western Pacific. Subsequently, these territories had become League of Nations Protectorates: Dutch New Guinea, Australian Papua and New Guinea, New Hebrides Condominium, British Solomon Islands Protectorate, New Zealand Protectorate of Western Samoa, among many others.

The accidents of western contact had greatly determined island development and cultural impact. For example, the Samoan peoples inhabited two major

5B

adjacent islands separated by some eighty miles. Western Samoa, with only a brief German occupation and a laissez-faire New Zealand administration, had maintained its strong indigenous culture. In contrast, American Samoa on the east, purchased from the Germans by America in 1900 as a coaling station for the U.S. Navy, was truly an American colony, with every son hoping to grow up and join the navy.

The New Hebrides was another oddity. Of dual British and French administration, it had completely separate post offices, police stations, and other service facilities. Two independent administrators and staffs maintained strict distance from each other, emphasizing their own versions of respective pomp and circumstance. The British Resident, for example, was escorted aboard his decked-out rowboat taking him to lunch daily at his off-shore residence, while his French colleague was provided a motorcade to his noon meal on shore.

An especially interesting finding from my research, later to be verified by on-site observation, was the German village health organization in Papua/New Guinea. At the turn of the 20th century, the Germans had developed a system of trained village health leaders, known as "tultuls". A medical tultul had some rudimentary health training and provided a focus for western medicine in the villages. The identifying uniform always consisted of a military white cap with a Red Cross above the black peak, along with a white sarong with a similar Red Cross. Considering that these had been issued prior to World War I, it was impressive to find the uniform in evidence during my travels, still worn with pride and obvious status, even though questionably related to any serious health function.

By today's standards, air travel was quite primitive: the twin engine Dakotas or cumbersome New Zealand seaplanes (PBY), known as the *flying boats*. The weather was always a factor with our schedules, takeoffs, and

61

landings, pilot discretion being paramount due to sporadic or nonexistent ground radio contact. The lack of airstrip lighting mandated day flights only. My flying experience was a constant adventure. The endless waiting at the Noumea airfield. The one hour return to town overnight to await later takeoff confirmation. Deplaning from the flying boat in a storm in Suva, Fiji, with row boats taking us ashore in rough seas. Accompanying a mission priest pilot in a two-seater craft to villages on the Sepik River in Papua, New Guinea. A mid-flight emergency return to Port Vila, New Hebrides at night, buzzing the town to alert cars to light up the airstrip with headlights for the descent through mountainous terrain.

I began this adventure with a western swing through Papua/New Guinea, the Solomon Islands, and Dutch New Guinea. To reach Papua, New Guinea from New Caledonia required a trip to Sydney and then an overnight flight to Port Moresby where there was a striking contrast between the mixed population of Europeans and Papuans in native dress. Reminders of the pre-World War I German days were evident in the towns of Finchaven and Lae on the east. Mt. Hagen natives in the central highlands displayed their Bird-of-Paradise plumes and little else. Among the villages on the Sepik River the tultuls still proudly displayed their official status with well-worn hats and sarongs.

The British Solomon Islands Protectorate offered a vivid reminder of World War II. Downed airplanes in the jungle; masses of navy equipment scuttled in harbors rimmed with beautiful sandy beaches; a British presence well-defined in the few settled outposts such as Honiara, the capital. As I toured the area with my trainee from the course, the possibility of making any serious health education or community organization in-roads began to appear remote indeed. I began experiencing an increasing sense of unreality and futility about the practicality of the course, as well as the sincerity of the Commission's effort. The Western occupying powers were simply making an impression on the international stage, while the fires of local independence movements were being lit. For this one frustrated health educator caught up in the process, this atmosphere ignited my latent feelings of inadequacy and failure at not being a trained physician with a clear-cut, independent professional role of my own.

Dutch New Guinea was a virtually untouched primitive wilderness apart from the administrative center at Biak (now Jayapura) and Fakfak. Fakfak was an outpost reached only by small plane and located on the far southwestern part of the island. It was inhabited by missionaries and an indigenous population totally cut off from the outside world. My student/trainee was highly motivated and anxious to put his new training into practical use, but, realistically, what could a health education program do in a situation such as this?

The old gaping wound of being a medical school reject resurfaced again as my subsequent Pacific travels unfolded. We headed eastward to Tahiti which involved three days from Auckland, New Zealand by *flying boat* via Suva, Fiji, Apia, Western Samoa, and Rarotonga, Cook Islands.

Tahiti was the South Seas of everyone's dream: a perimeter of beautiful sand beaches with gorgeous green hills in the center; a lagoon filled with world class yachts; a waterfront that was a conglomeration of bars, Chinese shops, and open restaurants; and a strong French influence - the music, the dancing, and the much heralded Tahitian women. There was sophistication in Tahiti far beyond anything we had seen in the Western Pacific. The two weeks' stay in Tahiti until our next return flight enabled us to visit Bora Bora and other outlying islands. This time was like being on a spectacular holiday.

Visits to Western and American Samoa revealed a

63

cultural divide far greater than the eighty miles separating these two island groups. This stop, in some ways, irrevocably changed my life. Western Samoa had retained its deep cultural heritage in spite of the pre-World War I German influence. We experienced the paramount importance of village leadership and the rituals of the "talking" ceremony while sipping kava, the native coconut brew. We slept in the traditional fale, an open round thatch structure, and were even provided with a large four-poster brass bed for all to see. This strong culture had attracted a final resting place for the exiled Robert Louis Stevenson, whose grave we visited at the residence of the New Zealand Governor General.

American Samoa had become "American" since its purchase from the Germans in 1900 as a port for the U.S. Navy. The dream of every American Samoan boy was to enlist and of every family to have some navy connection. My observation of the American hospital in Pago Pago, together with its well-organized public health program under the single direction of a physician from Boston, reinforced a smoldering hunger for the kind of medical training that could make this possible for me.

The rough sea voyage back to Western Samoa gave me little time to mull over the impact of this experience just then as the roasted pig we had been given at send-off added to my struggle with massive seasickness. As it turned out, the closed-in weather at Apia, the capital, prevented onward western flight. Days of continuous rain and the comfort of Aggie Grey's Hotel, famous from the writings of Somerset Maugham and others, were to provide the setting for some serious thinking and self-evaluation. Medical school was very much on my mind. The spectacular travel vistas could not cover over the void that had, once again, re-opened.

As the rain resounded off the tin roofs in Apia, I drafted a letter to Dr. Aura E. Severinghaus, the Dean at

Columbia University College of Physicians and Surgeons. How I could have remembered his name or what could have moved me to choose that lofty place of learning is beyond my comprehension to this day. I wrote in detail to the doctor a synopsis of my activities in the nine years since my days at Columbia College. I continued to express my need in becoming a physician. When we returned to Noumea some days later, I reviewed the letter and mailed it, this in spite of Barbara's doubts about the wisdom of once again applying to medical school.

A reply from New York *did* arrive a few weeks later suggesting that I visit Dean Severinghaus upon our return to the States.

Nearing completion of my one-year assignment, the timing of this correspondence was fortuitous. WHO and members of the Commission asked me to stay on. Continuing to roam the Pacific would certainly have been pleasant, but my travels had convinced me that there was little I could accomplish professionally. Instead, I decided to return to the interrupted fellowship at Yale.

Medical school was now very much on my mind.

CHAPTER 6
PHYSICIAN in the MAKING

Completing a 'round the world' circuit, Barbara and I returned to the states via Europe, making brief visits to Italy and Holland. Once again, we took up residence in New Haven, and soon after I made my way to the Columbia University College of Physicians and Surgeons in New York City. With eyes glazed over and a tingling, radiating feeling throughout my entire body, I anxiously entered the P&S building. I was relieved to find Dean Severinghaus to be a man both warm and relaxed. Kindly, grey-haired and be-speckled, Severinghaus spoke with nostalgia of his early professional years in China organizing a medical school. We soon established a bond of common interest relating to our overseas experiences. His litany of the many steps ahead for me in my pursuit of medical school acceptance made it clear that it would not be easy. Nevertheless, he was encouraging.

An Admission's Committee interview some weeks later indicated that he had put in a good word for me.

The application process involved obtaining past records, college transcripts, and becoming reacquainted with my old Columbia College advisor, a professor of English. He was astonished to see me going through the medical school admissions process yet another time and had some serious doubts about it. I persevered and did my best on the day-long admissions exams. These tests were

67

thoroughly disheartening. Largely on Barbara's suggestion, I also submitted applications to Harvard and Yale. I figured I might just as well shoot for the best on what surely would be my last attempt to become a doctor.

My life at this time functioned in a kind of suspended animation, with much of my focus being on medical school, and only a small residua left for my graduate studies at Yale. In the year before our South Pacific travels, I had completed my Master's Degree in Sociology and passed the language requirements in French and German and the Ph.D. qualifying exams. But I still had some course work to complete as well as the looming dissertation. My inclination was to do a study of the old German tultul system in New Guinea as it related to village structure and organization. Although it would have been lots of fun, a return trip to New Guinea to collect interview data would have been too impractical and unreasonably disruptive, especially with the possibility of medical school in the big picture.

Instead, I decided to be reasonable and approach the dissertation as a requirement to be completed in the least complicated manner possible. The sociologic concept of "sanctions" had come to interest me, and I settled on studying its application in how the New Haven Health Department dealt with infractions of health regulations among differing socioeconomic groups in the city. I hypothesized that one would find an inverse relation between social class and action of the health department. The value of this project lay in the easy accessibility of records requiring review – a major task that occupied much of my time in the months after our return from the Pacific. The job had a soporific effect, as well, while I awaited news about medical school.

On the morning of Monday, December 5, 1958, I headed out for my usual perch at the health department, stopping at the Yale post office to pick up my mail. The

6A

small, thin envelope with a Columbia University return address jolted my early morning sensibilities. A rush of nervousness made me fumble as I opened the envelope. And there it was. I had been accepted to P&S for the class of 1963. I ran home to tell Barbara.

"Oh, that's great," Barbara replied. She seemed slightly ambivalent while listening to me excitedly read the letter. She gave me a hug nonetheless. She then reminded me about her father's warning against her ever marrying a doctor. She sighed, "Of course, I did listen to him and didn't marry a doctor. But once you wrote that letter back in Apia, I knew that this *could* finally happen."

While Barbara was able to go off to work that morning at a New Haven department store, I simply could not settle down for the day. Instead, I decided to drive to New York. I headed straight for the Columbia campus and the premed bulletin board. There was the list of the names of this year's students heading to P&S from Columbia College - with my name there among the others! I happened to stumble upon a couple of my lucky fellow associates reading the list and overheard murmurs of, "Who the heck is this guy, Scherzer?"

Thus began the remnants of a lame duck year at Yale, and of making preparations for a new life ahead. I did go forward with the dissertation and even had a first draft typed. My findings were predictable: social class indeed weighed heavily on the type and severity of penalties levied by the health department for infractions. It was not very exciting stuff compared with the dizzying, and to some, mad pursuit of a medical career after all I had already done. *To this day that draft dissertation continues to gather dust in my attic.*

Getting ready for medical school became all-absorbing. After the initial buzz from the drama of my acceptance, I then began to develop a severe case of "cold feet". Should I really put Barbara and myself through all

71

this? Am I capable?

I decided to go to Washington and get the advice of Ted Butterworth, a friend in the Division of Public Health Education at the Public Health Service, a man I had known from my old Burma days. He could not have been more supportive. He put my mind to rest.

A few months later, a cable arrived from the WHO regional headquarters in New Delhi offering me the position of Regional Health Education Advisor for all of Southeast Asia! The exquisite timing for this opportunity *just as I was about to permanently change my life* suggested that Divine intervention was testing my resolve. Two very separate paths suddenly lay before me.

I did not hesitate for a moment.

After finishing out the academic year at Yale, my Aunt Henny, who lived on Washington Heights, came to our rescue and helped us find a spacious fifth floor walk-up apartment just across from the medical school. On moving-in day, I crossed paths with someone moving out. At age 29, he had just completed an ob/gyn residency and was now going into practice. Stunned at hearing my own statistics - being almost 31 and at a beginner's level - he just shook his head in disbelief and walked away in astonishment.

Barbara and I first became acquainted with some of the one hundred twenty members of my freshman class at several get-together events in late summer 1959. Many of them were very young, quite aloof, desperately immature, with few social graces, and with no real interest in reaching out beyond peers who had similar geographical or educational backgrounds and with whom they could immediately identify. With some, not a hint of recognition nor a change of facial expression would ever greet me upon their ever bumping into me over the following four years. With others, given time, this would change. I was even voted a class officer in my third year of medical

72

6B

school. There were a couple of *seniors* like myself - not quite my age. One was African (from Ghana) with whom I developed a strong friendship, as well as several of the women students - the ten percent quota numbering twelve women - including one of Chinese ancestry. *(This number is in sharp contrast to today's classes in which women may be in the majority.)* At an organizational meeting, Dean Severinghaus likened us to a symphony orchestra. When he spoke of the need for both first and second fiddles, I couldn't help feeling a personal reference to my being located in the latter section of this orchestra. The two of us never did have another direct conversation. Yet on occasion during my medical school years, our eyes would meet and he would acknowledge our silent bond with a nod.

Overall, this was clearly an intense, competitive group, ready for a jump-start and a fast getaway. My anomalous position surfaced on the very first day in biochemistry lab where everyone (students and faculty alike) wore lab coats. When a fellow student respectfully asked if I could help with one of the experiments, I spent an embarrassing few minutes explaining to him our co-equal status. It wasn't amusing at the time as I, too, had serious problems dealing with this new and uncharted territory.

First year quickly developed for me into an ever-deepening whirl of confusion. I constantly struggled to keep afloat with the maze of overwhelming material from the basic sciences (anatomy, biochemistry, and physiology), made much more difficult without clinical correlation. Exams involved mostly essay questions using the famous blue books – sheets of lined paper enclosed in blue covers - standard in college courses at the time, and pre-dating the electronic multiple choice format now in vogue. My college background in chemistry, a review course taken in New Haven, and frequent crib sessions

75

with two fellow students, helped ease me through biochemistry. Gross dissection of the cadaver (a withered elderly woman) by our four member team didn't give me a hint of what to study for exams, though the grim experience provided an oddly positive opportunity in forming special friendships with the team members. Physiology put me on another planet. An end of term conference with concerned and caring department staff hinted at what to study for the exam, and, in the end, they passed me more on faith in my future than current performance. It was a nightmare of a year, with frequent studying through the night - night after night. And while my glazed-over eyes were too tired to stray very far from a textbook during a quiet moment in the day, many of my fellow students took their leisure with card games in the student lounge! I have often wondered how Barbara was able to live through it.

With the summer off working for a private foundation doing a research study on childhood accidents, I eased into the next phase that would involve continuous medical school studies and a future medical school experience that would no longer include summer vacations.

Second year was just as strenuous, but I felt more secure, and although lost in clinical pathology, I received much needed help from the faculty (literally my chronological contemporaries) who took pity on me. A summer pathology elective included research on the effect of thymectomy on C3H mice and led to my first scientific publication.

By the third year, a veil began to lift for me as basic science now became correlated with clinical exposure to patients. That first night call of a patient admitted with pneumonia brought me alongside the intern and resident into the doctor's world of history and initial examination, and initiated me into the rite of completing blood and urine tests for immediate study. The traditional student

76

case presentation to the professor of medicine that took place later in the year was a make-or-break event that could mean not only a pass or fail difference, but could later affect internship acceptance. Barbara drilled me all night long in presenting and showing pathology slides of my patient with actinomycosis, a rare fungal pneumonia. It was a terrifying experience at the bedside in a big open ward with all the patients and fellow students focused on me, but there was relief and joy when all went well. Exposure to various surgical and other medical specialties during the year, including pediatrics, still did not sway me into any particular area of preference.

It is said that a doctor never knows more than when he is a senior in medical school. And this, of course, quickly changes when exposed to the real world. But that last year did move along particularly well, capped by the birth of Lisa, our first child, which occurred while I was on ob/gyn rotation. My original idea of a career in preventive medicine and public health began to fade as I became more aware of a need to be a clinician and preserve all my hard-won medical knowledge. A life in public health and administration would have been a retreat from all my medical studies completed and all my knowledge gained. Further contact with clinical pediatrics convinced me to move in that direction for my internship.

Graduation is always a grand affair at Columbia. Cloaked now in academic garb with the traditional green stripes of medicine, I came down the steps of Butler Library and faced the huge crowd of spectators seated in South Field. I had been though this ceremony several times before and now certainly qualified as a veteran on this campus.

The later - *more private and intimate* - oath-taking ceremony held uptown in the garden of P & S was another matter. Standing there and swearing to uphold the ageless traditions of Hippocrates was a culmination of all those

77

years of frustration and yearning. In the end, I could hardly believe that it had happened - I had finally become a physician.

In retrospect, I have many thoughts on the medical school pedagogy of the day to which we were all exposed. While being extremely fortunate in attending P & S which was a top ranking US medical school, its curriculum rigidly followed the dictates laid down from recommendations that dated from the 1916 Flexner Commission: basic sciences first; application and clinical correlation later. Moreover, the narrow, egocentric focus of the lofty physician carefully guarding his armamentarium of knowledge with the hospital as an impregnable fortress was much in evidence. Emphasis was on disease rather than on health - the specific organ involved instead of the whole person - curative rather than preventive services - the hospital as the privileged place where the doctor treated his patient, in place of the community roots of illness. Indeed, the fourth year course in preventive medicine had a demanding curriculum in public health infectious and parasitic diseases, but provided little attention to prevention, community health, or wellness. In a surreptitious way, four years at one of the finest US medical schools had sent us off, not only with the basic knowledge on which to function professionally, but perhaps more importantly, sent us into the accepted medical tradition at the time. Only years of further training, life experience, and practice would mold and shape how each of us would eventually function as a physician.

I also marvel at the primitive state of our basic scientific concepts at the time. The genetic revolution of the double helix, DNA, RNA, were yet to come; we worked only with traditional genetics to understand disease patterns; immunology was in its infancy. Nonetheless, the med school program had been a jam-packed four years of learning. In perspective, it is clear that medical knowledge and all scientific information are always in a time warp and in a constant state of flux and change. Perhaps the true worth of my quality medical education lay in the preparation it gave me to constantly build on what I had been taught and to keep re-learning. In a real sense, medical school started me on a path of life-long self-education that continues to this day.

The next steps in this process would be the maturing years of internship and the residency that followed.

CHAPTER 7
FINDING MY DIRECTION

A fourth floor walk-up apartment located at 1303 York Avenue on the fashionable East Side of Manhattan, across the street from New York Hospital. That was our family's next move in my new status as Intern in Pediatrics at Cornell Medical Center. At P&S, some of my fellow students had considered this move downtown to be the height of treachery, as Columbia and Cornell were traditional archrivals. Columbia, however, did not have a pediatrics internship at the time, and so I had no alternative but to apply for internships elsewhere. A memorable incident during my application process at Cornell was my interview with Professor Charlie Bauer. Bauer had been a Columbia College classmate of mine and would later become a faculty colleague.

The lofty central tower of New York Hospital - Cornell Medical Center and its adjoining structures with their art-deco windows overlooking the East River - evoked for one a sense of medical majesty and authority. This feeling of the total medical community was further heightened by the imposing adjacent campus of Rockefeller University and the Memorial Sloan Kettering Medical Center. For me, this transition from the much larger Columbia Presbyterian Medical Center seemed like a move to a smaller, more compact medical universe.

Any possible *know-it-all* smirks and conceits from my

senior medical school days vanished quickly as I became immersed in this new reality as an intern working every other night and every other weekend. That very year marked the first time ever that Cornell paid an annual stipend ($1000) to its interns. Most hospitals at the time provided room and board only, considering the internship experience a privileged and integral part of training, rather than recognizing it as a form of indentured service. There was less intense patient demand due to the surrounding upscale referral neighborhood, and together with the considerable supervision by faculty, Cornell provided a strong teaching experience without the burdensome survival demands frequently found in a city hospital.

After this busy and successful year interning, a time which included publication of a paper on the new antibiotic, ampicillin, I decided to stay on for an additional two-year Pediatric residency at Cornell. It seemed the most practical means of completing requirements for Board certification in pediatrics. I also turned down the offer of an additional year as Chief Resident. Supervisory responsibilities of junior house staff and the teaching of medical students in those years rounded out my training. My second daughter, Andrea, was born at New York Hospital. We now had heirs from both of my training hospitals.

The most significant experience in all of my time at Cornell training was attending the Cerebral Palsy Clinic at the Hospital for Special Surgery and meeting Dr. William Cooper, its Director. Upon first meeting Cooper, his icy blue eyes and shiny bald head immediately captured my attention. He sat there in his conference room enthroned at the head of two rows. On the one side sat the medical students, residents and ancillary staff, therapists, social workers, psychologists. On the other side sat the parents. Patients were brought in by wheelchair, sometimes with walkers or crutches, with a few occasionally ambulating

7A

independently. The patients approached Dr. Cooper individually from a waiting area on the far side, across the length of the therapy room, moving down the aisle composed of observing medical and paramedical personnel. Dr. Cooper had each individual's chart in hand from which he would read pertinent notes to the assembled, much as a nobleman might address his subjects. His manner was soft, a smile often present, as he demonstrated pertinent features of the patient, reported on progress, and made recommendations for further management. During the entire process, the staff maintained reverent, and in some instances, devotional attention.

It was my first exposure as a physician to patients having cerebral palsy, and a critical period as I evaluated each new medical experience for clues to my medical future. I was immediately drawn to this population of infants and young children who manifested a broad range of motor disabilities. Some were totally involved and confined in wheelchairs. Others had only mild conditions, perhaps slightly affecting the use of a hand, or merely reducing cosmetic quality of gait.

Parental involvement and concern also impressed me greatly. From their questions addressed to Dr. Cooper, I could see something of the enormous impact a chronic condition had on a family. I had already learned how any childhood illness affects the caregivers. But with a life-long problem like cerebral palsy, everyone was involved. Bill Cooper paid very close attention to parental concerns and often anticipated the need for information, directions, and reassurance. Though an orthopedic surgeon, he appeared more focused on how the family was coping or the child functioning than on the need for a surgical procedure. The family would go away from their audience with Cooper generally given as much direction as to improving their child's school performance as to the need

85

for more therapy.

The row of paramedical staff across the aisle revealed to me a completely new dimension in medical care. The physical therapists, occupational therapists, speech therapists, psychologists, and social workers who eagerly followed Dr. Cooper's presentations were obviously an integral part of the team much needed to manage these patients. I also heard then about the orthotists, prosthetists, special equipment vendors, all who also played an important part offstage, as it were. In addition, the whole area of education came into play, regular and special education teachers, vocational training specialists, and recreational therapists, comprising a cadre of professionals whose impact required at least equal billing with the medical and paramedical staff. It was quite an array of individuals who, at some point, would influence development of the child with cerebral palsy.

And then there was Bill Cooper himself. His imperious posture at the center of attention both repelled and attracted me. On first contact, this image of a medieval court with devoted subjects paying homage to their prince put me off slightly, but still, his manner was soft and his demeanor pleasant. He obviously cared primarily about the broad concerns of his patients rather than just their medical requirements. After he gave a resume from the patient's chart, the emphasis was always on general developmental issues, like school, self-care, managing with public transportation, instead of on the next operation. He would turn to the staff for suggestions and contributions about management. There seemed to be a very good back and forth exchange between the spectators' seats and Dr. Cooper's place of command.

Added to this, was Cooper's interaction with accompanying parents. They stood by and waited as the chart was read and always deferred to Dr. Cooper while he commented with the staff. But I noted that he was

86

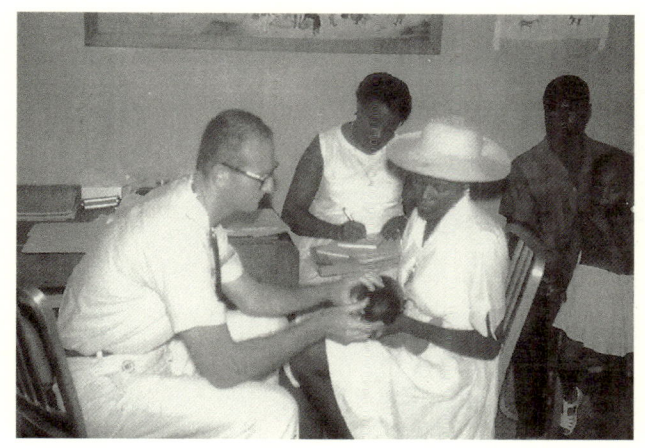

7B

particularly caring with the parent, usually inquiring about other family members whom he frequently knew well from years of contact. Often the dialogue with staff enlarged to include the mother or other caregivers. If there were differences of opinion, Dr. Cooper resolved the matter quickly in his role of a totally *in control* yet beneficent healer. Here, in a real sense, the parent was clearly a functioning member of the team and very much included in the drama affecting his or her child. It was a very new experience for me and one fascinating to watch.

After that first visit I began a regular weekly schedule at the clinic. My first impression of Dr. Cooper and his overwhelmingly powerful personality was only reinforced with further contact. We soon became personally acquainted. He gave me patient assignments and responsibilities far beyond my training and experience at the time.

***

During my senior year of residency, I worked on a two-month rotation at the Hospital Albert Schweitzer in Deschapelles, Haiti. During our stay there, Barbara and I pondered the possibility of a future overseas career for our family. Lisa was then 2 years old and Andrea 6 months. Getting to know the founders, Larry and Gwen Mellon, and participating in this impressive hospital experience in this impoverished area provided a temptation to continue on the path of global pediatrics. The Haitian experience clearly confirmed our strong interest in international travel and the rewards of having an in-depth experience with a local area and its people. However, the transient nature of relationships, both between colleagues and hosts and the uncertainty of future assignments in an overseas setting, led us to decide against an international career.

On our return to Cornell I found myself accepting three positions. The first assignment was as the Assistant

89

Medical Director of the Nassau County Cerebral Palsy Center (UCP), the place where Dr. Cooper had served as Medical Director for many years. I was also going to work as an attending pediatrician in the CP Clinic at the Hospital for Special Surgery. And finally, I was to perform clinic duties at Cornell as Assistant Professor of Pediatrics. These decisions led to my ultimately focusing on the child with handicaps, an uncharted territory at the time with no subspecialty status.

Successfully completing multitudes of examinations marked my passage from medical student to Doctor of Medicine and to New York State licensure. The final step to certification as a pediatrician by the American Board of Pediatrics, however, was elusive. I had no difficulty with the written portion but failed the oral exam, initially taken in New Orleans, and then re-taken in Nashville. I was devastated to have come this far and have my status as a specialist now dangling in limbo. I spent eighteen months of uncertainty with haunting visions of my languishing somewhere, a frustrated GP for the rest of my days. These visions filled every waking moment of my life until I finally passed the orals satisfactorily in Chicago. It was another rite of passage. Soon after, Martha, our third child, was born at New York Hospital.

My responsibilities at Cornell included the general pediatric outpatient services and also attending the Developmental Disorders Clinic (DDC) funded in part by the March of Dimes Foundation. I found myself quickly gravitating to the children with multiple disorders and with congenital anomalies in the DDC, and becoming particularly interested in those with spina bifida (SB). I found it fascinating to work with the multi-system problems of these children, requiring both services from many specialties as well as the need for unified, coordinated care. The clinic fast became the focus for SB for the entire New York metropolitan area. Ultimately,

90

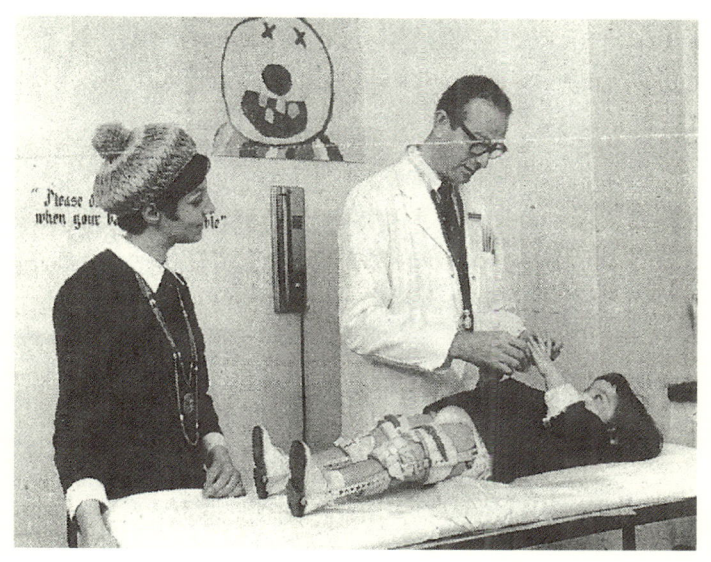

7C

neurology, neurosurgery, orthopedics, urology, and psychiatry specialties attended the clinic regularly and provided a medical home for these children. Sessions were held for parents and adolescents, as well. The heightened clinic activity led to its designation as the Pediatric Habilitation Clinic, and I ultimately became Director of a new Division of Pediatric Habilitation within the Department of Pediatrics. On recommendation of a colleague, I was also designated Editor of the *Pediatric Habilitation Series* for Marcel Dekker Book Publishers, which ultimately produced fourteen titles.

When I began my work at the Nassau County Cerebral Palsy Center, I was unaware that I would be replacing the incumbent clinic director - a man whom Dr. Cooper intended to remove either because he had become too popular, or perhaps, was a professional rival. The pressure and anxiety caused by this removal of my predecessor made my transition from pediatric resident to practitioner a complicated one. The clinic director strongly resisted the dismissal. I was then caught unawares between two camps of parents either objecting to or supporting the change. While attending a two-week training course in Cerebral Palsy by Dr. Meyer Perlstein at the Cook County Graduate School of Medicine in Chicago, Dr. Cooper had me fly to New York for an appearance at the UCP Annual Meeting in order to support his decision. I then returned immediately by *red eye* to Chicago and continued my course.

Somehow, I survived that difficult period and went on to become immersed in the care and treatment of over 1000 children and adults with cerebral palsy at the Center.

Shortly after taking over at UCP, Dr. Cooper had me assume an additional assignment that reflected his varied interests and contacts. He was among the early pioneers who advocated health services and therapy in the public schools for children with handicaps. This was long before

93

passage of national legislation for children with disabilities. In the late 1950s, he had implemented classes specifically for children with physical disabilities in New York City. By the time I came along, he had become the coordinator of the program administered by the Department of Health. The pattern of spreading his influence through appointment of trusted surrogates soon extended to me, and I became a part-time school physician in one of these units at P.S. 87 in Manhattan, in addition to my responsibilities at Cornell, the HSS CP Clinic, and UCP Nassau. It was another example of Dr. Cooper broadening the scope of my experience in direct line with his multi-dimensional concepts about the needs of the handicapped child. Again the emphasis was on social and educational services other than medical ones - a far-ranging approach then as now. Taking on this assignment illustrated how much my activities and my time were being stretched in many directions.

Ultimately, it became apparent that Bill Cooper's political manipulations had greatly reduced his stature and standing with the board of directors at UCP Nassau. Several years after my appointment he was *elevated* to a consultant position. I then replaced him as Medical Director. It was ironic that the junior who succeeded him had come along just at a time when his status as the omnipotent physician could no longer be tolerated. Dr. Cooper had obviously exerted an enormous influence on my professional life. He also influenced strongly our family's life as I learned about his summer home in Westhampton Beach on the East End of Long Island to which he drove after his Friday afternoons at the CP Center. That led me to find a summer place in Hampton Bays, as well, where we eventually became full-time residents. In spite of his strong professional stature, his demanding ego was often difficult to deal with and is perhaps the reason his photo was never included along

94

with those of my teachers Herb Walker and Aura Severinghaus, photos that have a prominent place on my desk.

Shortly after beginning my position at the Nassau UCP, I attended my first Annual Meeting of the American Academy of Cerebral Palsy in New Orleans. Presentations by proponents of the most popular systems of physical and occupational therapy at the time drew a very large attendance and quickly initiated me into this specialized field. Scientific papers and presentations opened up areas of possible research, and the instructional courses provided much needed training not found elsewhere at the time. I subsequently attended every annual meeting, became actively involved in the Academy, served as its President in 1985-1986, started the International Affairs and Advocacy Committees, became Historian in 2009, and received its Lifetime Achievement Award in 2011.

Simultaneous involvement in other widespread activities dealing with the child with handicaps quickly became the pattern of my professional development. More was to come.

CHAPTER 8
BRANCHING OUT

In 1964-1965 New York City experienced a near epidemic of congenital rubella involving large numbers of pregnant women. The possible range of disabilities among affected infants included any combination of challenges including cataracts, deafness, cardiac defects, intellectual deficit, and cerebral palsy. By 1969-1970, these affected children became eligible for school, however there was no system in place to provide for their multiple needs.

As a physician at P.S. 87 providing services for children with cerebral palsy and other physical handicapping conditions during this period, I made periodic evaluations and supervised outside of the classroom therapy treatments. At the time this "medical model" was considered to be far advanced, enabling attendance by children who otherwise would have been excluded by virtue of their disability. There were similar programs for those with several other specific conditions including blindness, deafness, intellectual deficit, and emotional disabilities. Children were rigidly assigned on the basis of their disability with staff oriented toward the needs of the specific condition. The congenital rubella children who first became eligible for kindergarten in 1969 confounded this system because so many of them had a multiplicity of developmental problems. Several top school administrators were far-sighted enough to see a

97

looming problem in providing for these youngsters and obtained Federal funds to establish a new school approach. Dr. Edmund Horan was appointed director to develop the program.

Ed had been a teacher of children with intellectual deficit for many years. He never lost focus on their everyday needs nor of the difficulties confronting the staff who had chosen to work with this group. Of medium build, Ed appeared short and was a bit stocky. His soft spoken, kindly manner was his trademark. No one ever saw him angry or negative. His shiny bald pate crowned prominent gray sideburns, and set off a soft Irish smile. The ever-present stream of smoke from his pipe made him easy to locate and a ready caricature for the cartoonist's pen. He took his new assignment seriously, wanted to learn all about these new kids with congenital rubella, and was determined to put together a professional staff that could meet the multiple needs they would face.

For some time Ed Horan had been aware of the existing, narrowly-focused, medical model providing only services for children with specific individual handicaps. He sensed the need for a new and more comprehensive system, one which would closely integrate medical and therapy services with special education, social service, recreation, and family support. He gathered around him a team of experienced professionals who would reflect this approach. Because of my work with cerebral palsy, I was asked to become the medical consultant for the original organizing group.

Those early introductory meetings gave me a taste of the quiet, effective manner in which Dr. Horan worked to shape our mission and purpose. He was an excellent listener and tried to clearly understand everyone's point of view. Differences of opinion among the consultants were used as a means for general debate and discussion.

8A

He instilled in us a new dimension of operation. Over and over again he would say, "The school experience for these kids has to focus on developing life skills. But don't forget that many will always remain totally dependent. The years they spend in school may be the best ones they will ever have. So it's our job not only to educate, but to make their time with us a great experience."

Those first few months taught me a great deal about the logistics of screening children, locating a school building site, and arranging the needed special busing. I was able to arrange screening of new entrants with the child neurologist in the Out-Patient Clinic at New York Hospital. Ed saw to it that all of us were totally involved in each of these aspects. The obstacles were many, mostly involving the bureaucracy of the Board of Education itself. While Ed Horan never lost his cool, he many times came back from the meetings "downtown" with less than his usual smile, biting harder on his pipe. The former insider had himself become ensnared in a web of administrative tangle.

But the Center for Children with Multiple Handicaps (CCMH) did open on Park Avenue at 106th Street in Harlem, located in a renovated former film storage building adjacent to the elevated railroad tracks. It quickly became a magnet for children bussed from all boroughs of the city. As promised, Horan made the school day a special experience for these kids, with classroom and therapy sessions interspersed with music and art, field trips, and imported cultural activities. For many, music was truly a universal language. I remember Jeannie, our music teacher, putting together a chorus of some of the most handicapped youngsters. She literally pulled out whatever talents they had and made a cohesive group that, on occasion, brought their talent to other schools. I have a photo of Ed taking a turn leading the group. I look at it every once in a while to remind myself of the deep joy and satisfaction mirrored on his face.

Virtually every staff member was involved with the children. Even Clara, our cook, not only prepared snacks and lunches, but came around to help with the dining, and often joined in the chorus or participated on stage in one of the plays. It was typical that we all attended Clara's wedding reception, hosted of course, by Ed Horan.

The center had been funded as a two year Federal demonstration center. There was some nervousness among us when the time came for renewal. Many parents had become actively involved in the school and were alerted by Ed to exert their influence within the City. Naturally, he was totally immersed in the whole budgeting process. Just when everything seemed to be moving along smoothly, a parent called Ed to indicate that the budget request for continuation of the school had been rejected. Ed called a meeting to let us know of this decision. For all of us there, the meeting seemed like a wake for a young child who had great promise.

We then threw away our self-pity and mobilized the parents. They literally bombarded City Hall with calls and petitions and that prompted a decision to have a public hearing on our funding. I remember worrying about this all day as I went about my hospital work. Shortly after I returned home for dinner, Ed called.

Anxiety and tension in his voice were clear indications that everything was still uncertain. "Al, they're still objecting about taking us on the regular budget," he said. "I don't think we've been able to convince them that these kinds of kids are going to be around for a long time. The Board is used to the old rigid disability classifications and doesn't want to hear about anything else they don't know..."

He faltered.

It was a call of desperation, a call for my assistance.

102

8B

Over those past two years there had been so many crises that had required us to work together under the most unusual circumstances, but this one capped them all. Our survival was at stake. Without further comment, I told him I would be there.

After a hurried car trip downtown at the end of rush hour, I remember my face being flushed as I entered the Board of Estimate Hall. A large crowd of familiar *but unsmiling* faces filled the seats facing the inquiring commissioners. The presence of both parents and staff was certainly expected, but I was much surprised to see a number of our students, including some of the most severely involved, in attendance. It was very late in the day. Many were tired or distracted. A worried-looking Ed Horan was on the podium making his plea for a permanent school budget.

In my remarks that followed, I emphasized that we were demanding the permanent continuation of a program that had been proven to be effective. We demanded also that it would not simply be for the rubella kids, but for all children with multiple disabilities. I had brought the figures with me showing that the new trend in care of high-risk newborns through increasing use of Neonatal Intensive Care Units (NICU) had resulted in improved survival; that we should now anticipate and plan for a significant increase in children with multiple disabilities in our school system. I emphasized that the program we had demonstrated at the CCMH should be expanded throughout the City to meet these anticipated needs.

Several days of nail-biting uncertainty followed. I was in the middle of a screening meeting when Ed burst in with a face more crimson than I had ever seen. Our funding had been reinstated! We were now included in the regular, permanent budget!

The hugs, the tears of joy gave us all an escape from those days and weeks of tension. A special school assembly commemorated the victory and Jeannie had the chorus do a new song for the occasion.

Over the next ten years, Ed would be responsible for developing similar units in all boroughs of the City. These ultimately became integrated into the regular NYC school system organization. By this time, new federal laws had been enacted mandating education for all children with handicaps, irrespective of disability. Once again my activities multiplied as I became medical director of these new centers and Medical Director of the Division of Special Education at the Board of Education.

Ed Horan's work also became greatly expanded and the struggles with administration never ceased. Sadly, we saw less and less of him. On the few occasions he attended our meetings the old smile was gone. There now was a decided tremor in his hands. His announcement about taking early retirement did not come as a surprise and we were glad to hear that, at last, he and his wife, Kay, would start to travel. He wanted to try his hand at painting, as well.

Sadly, it was not to be. Within a few months, Kay informed us that Ed had been diagnosed with lung cancer. He refused to see any of us in the hospital. Kay said it was his pride. I knew better. He just didn't want to cause us distress at our seeing him. At least the end came quickly. And then he was gone.

But not his work or his influence. We were determined to have his name displayed on the first demonstration center that had brought us all together. It did come to pass after the usual delays and the endless administrative struggles. Commuters can see it daily from the elevated tracks along Park Avenue as their trains approach the city: DR. EDMUND M. HORAN SCHOOL.

How could anyone ever know the extent of the devotion symbolized by those words?

How could anyone realize the legacy of his influence

which has enabled so many children with severe disabilities to become part of a meaningful school experience?

Those of us who joined with him and lived through the early developing years at CCMH are proud to have had a role in enabling today's special education programs become a seamless part of the entire school system.

CHAPTER 9
TURNING EAST

Increasing frustration in dealing with demands of the UCP Board of Directors led me to resign after a decade's work. I then became involved with child developmental problems in Eastern Long Island where I learned there was a serious lack of needed local services. By then, our family had made a permanent move from a spacious East Side apartment to what had been our summer home in Hampton Bays. My activities continued at the Cornell Medical Center, the New York City schools for children with multiple handicaps, and as consultant to the UCP of New York City. Two full days in the city with an overnight at the New York Athletic Club enabled me to juggle both town and country. Although now a New York City commuter, my activities at various times only increased: Chairman of the New York State American Academy of Pediatrics Committee on Children with Disabilities; member of the Riverhead Business Improvement District; elected member of the Riverhead Board of Education; President of the Eastern Long Island Audubon Society.

My local travels, personal interviews, and community surveys of the Eastern Long Island area quickly confirmed the need for available facilities for evaluation and treatment of children with disabilities. Families had been obliged to travel considerable distances west or into metropolitan New York for needed specialized medical

109

services. Teachers and social workers indicated that many children either had never received care or lacked adequate follow-up.

Convincing local doctors that there truly were children in need turned out to be more difficult than anticipated. My pediatric colleagues, in particular, told me they had not seen any kids with disabilities in their practice. None of the doctors discouraged me from pursuing possible involvement, but most thought that establishing such a specialty in the area was totally unnecessary and certainly would be unrewarding in every respect.

An attempt to interest Southampton Hospital in establishing a clinic for these children was rejected by its Chief of Pediatrics, again as something totally unnecessary. My efforts at Central Suffolk Hospital in Riverhead, however, proved more fruitful. A new young administrator sensed that my project could offer the possibility of improving much needed community involvement. He also accepted the studies indicating that a significant group of children in need had no access to services. Thus, the Child Habilitation Center (CHC) opened in 1976 amidst the general indifference of medical staff.

There was immediate community interest in the CHC and a demand for services! Children came from all areas of the East End. Those attending special education at the Board of Cooperative Education Services (BOCES) in Westhampton Beach, where I also served as consultant, were regularly bussed to the CHC. To meet the need, staff grew rapidly to include physical, occupational and speech therapists, social worker, and orthotist.

I became aware that some families preferred a private office to the clinic setting. Through contact with a local realtor I found a rectangular brick-faced building on Riverhead's Second Street, a location that I could afford. In the center of the small downtown business area just east

110

9

of the post office and adjacent to a landmark three-story house, the building was of historic interest as a leather factory and saddlery during World War II. There was easy access right off the street for patients in wheelchairs with a convenient parking area in the rear. And my new Child Habilitation Center was located just a mile from Central Suffolk Hospital. In time, patients would come to refer to me as *the Second Street Doc*.

Over the course of almost thirty years, I evaluated hundreds of local children through thousands of clinic and office visits. The first few months of activity brought out many curious, often timid families. Many times these families had children with significant physical disabilities such as cerebral palsy or spina bifida. Many had had no previous care or had been lost to follow-up years before. Often they had been discouraged from seeking treatment because of the past advice of professionals, because of distance to services, or due to personal problems.

When I arrived on the scene, these families were simply looking for what a new doc in the area could offer. For the first time in my experience I saw the "natural" outcome of completely untreated conditions: severe limb contractures from cerebral palsy; profound intellectual deficit in Down syndrome with hypothyroidism; spina bifida with recurrent urinary tract infections. Dealing with these problems challenged the limited local resources available and often required referrals for specialist care out of the area. I had to establish solid rapport with families to enable needed follow-through management.

This first wave of children with visible and obvious physical disabilities was then followed by those children with poorly controlled and inadequately monitored medical conditions such as seizure disorders.

Over the years, the emphasis has gradually shifted from low frequency, high morbidity conditions such as cerebral palsy and spina bifida, to high frequency, low

113

morbidity attention deficit disorders, autism, and learning disabilities. This epidemiologic trend has many roots and now predominates in the more affluent countries of the world. This trend has also greatly broadened the variety of conditions now confronting the field of Developmental Pediatrics.

In the course of grappling with management of the various medical and developmental conditions, I have become increasingly aware of their potential effect on the family. While it is obvious that any chronic disorder will have its impact on the affected child, the extent of parental interaction and the many forms it can take are not often or easily apparent. These reactions can follow a broad arc of emotions - total rejection, denial, guilt, fear of stigma, inaccurate understanding, feelings of betrayal, self-punishment, unrealistic expectations, demanding behavior, overprotection, and power conflicts to belated love, acceptance, and resignation. All of these interactions form an essential part of the disability itself requiring close scrutiny and attempts at resolution.

My deep interest in the problems as well as the accomplishments of my patients has led me to chronicle aspects of their lives to which I have been drawn. Through writing vignettes focusing on the patients themselves I was surprised to learn how family interaction has been predominant. This serendipitous finding was a reminder to me of how family dynamics can be a significant part of the developmental condition itself, as well as on the health and stability of those who surround the affected child.

I was grateful not to be discouraged by those who insisted that children with disabilities could not be found on the East End of Long Island. Strangely enough, many of the nay-sayers from the old days subsequently became major sources of referral for new patients. Perhaps my presence enabled some to accept a legitimate medical role in the care of these children, while others were relieved that someone else was willing to take on the responsibility. Ultimately, either as clinic physician or as *the Second Street Doc*, I had the satisfaction of attending to so very many of these children who previously had had few local resources for much needed services.

CHAPTER 10
A NEW ACADEMIC CAREER

By the mid-1990s, I decided that it was time to leave New York City and so, after thirty years, retired from Cornell as Clinical Professor Emeritus of Pediatrics. Shortly after, I also left my position as Medical Director for Special Education at the New York City Board of Education. For several years after, though, I did continue private practice of Developmental Pediatrics at my Second Street office, as well as my position as Medical Director at the Board of Cooperative Education Services (BOCES), and maintained the Child Habilitation Center at Central Suffolk Hospital, now Peconic Bay Medical Center, (PBMC) in Riverhead. I also continued to search for other possible opportunities that might be of interest, such as at the National Institutes of Health (NIH), UNICEF, WHO, and elsewhere.

In early 2003, with Barbara in residential care to better manage her failing health and her Alzheimer's disease, and, as a respite from her long illness, I made a return visit to Burma. It was wonderful to revisit Rangoon and find a city not greatly changed after all these years; to again see Taunggyi in the Northern Shan States now unrecognizable as a cramped, bustling city in contrast to the bucolic village I had known, and to experience Pagan for the first time.

It was in Rangoon that I unexpectedly met the current

Director of the Health Education Bureau - an agency which I had initiated fifty years previously! That my work had endured through all these years of Burmese political turmoil, well, that took some time to fully comprehend. It led me to more seriously explore possible international activities once again.

Health Volunteers Overseas (HVO), an international agency with focus on strengthening local teaching facilities, brought to my attention the program at the Angkor Hospital for Children (AHC) in Sean Reap, Cambodia, the only pediatric training center in the country. It had been founded in 1996 by Kenro Izu, a well-known Japanese-American photographer, who periodically photographed the nearby ancient ruins at Angkor Wat. He had become aware of the poor health quality for the local children and envisioned the need for a local pediatric training facility.

The death of Barbara in 2003 left a great void in my life. I viewed participating at AHC as an opportunity to return to the international scene.

During my first one-month AHC tour in 2004, the pediatricians-in-training were literally stunned at the concepts of orderly child development, the availability of clinical tools for very early identification of developmental delays and disabilities, and the benefits of early intervention. Great interest was piqued even though there were few available therapy or habilitation services in Cambodia. The training sessions were designed to kindle a foundation for the future provision of needed facilities as children became increasingly identified. The focus was placed on informing the family about the child's problem to help improve interaction and relationships and to provide assistance in early child care that would enhance development. Obviously, much research would be needed to better understand and positively deal with parental superstitions, misconceptions, and attitudes. Still, family

118

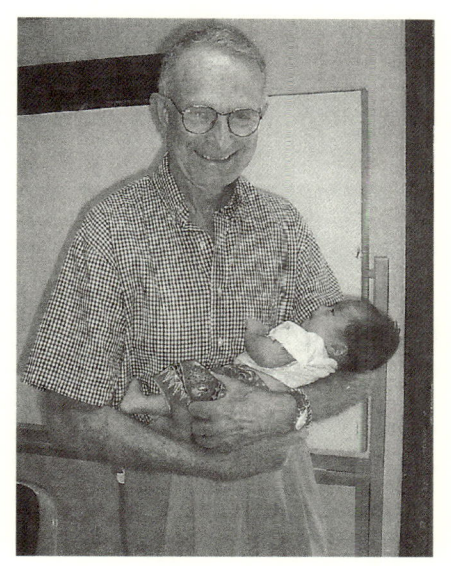

10

involvement was paramount, irrespective of available services, then or in the future. The theoretical concepts were carried over into the daily clinics and on regular in-patient rounds.

Following my first tour in Cambodia, I began to re-assess my practice and my professional future. The ever-increasing patient records from my private practice were becoming a concern for eventual accessibility and I turned to the Department of Pediatrics at Stony Brook in 2004 for a possible solution. My inquiry to the Chairman, Dr. Richard Fine, led to an unexpected offer from Stony Brook to rent my building, and, in addition, provided me a part-time faculty position. I also continued practice on Second Street along with other pediatricians. My patients at the Child Habilitation Center were urged to transfer to this new arrangement. Stony Brook encouraged me to continue annual monthly tours of AHC and I became mentor for third-year residents in a global pediatric elective, from 2005-2010.

My annual tours enabled me to become better acquainted with Cambodia: a poor rice-growing country with primitive village water and sanitary conditions unchanged from the distant past. Agriculture is dependent on the northerly flow of the Mekong River from China as it reverses and flows north during the rainy season and floods the paddy fields annually. Tonle Sap Lake, with its colorful floating villages in the center of the country, is a major fishing resource. Siem Reap, site of the AHC, in the north-west is becoming, in contrast, a bustling increasingly Westernized tourist town. On its edge are the ancient ruins of Angkor Wat with many temples built in the period between 800–1200 A.D., a period when Cambodia was the dominant power in the region. Phnom Penh, the capital in the south, is a major and quite Westernized city. Its royal palace and its museum of the Khmer Rouge days offers strong reminders of Cambodia's both ancient glorious past and its devastatingly horrific recent years.

AHC, in the central part of Siem Reap, is serviced by ever-present tuc-tucs and motor bikes that defy traffic lanes, bicycles, trucks, and increasingly, motor cars. The center's stucco buildings include an open outpatient waiting area, clinic, inpatient services and a medical education wing. Not infrequently, families travel for days and wait overnight to be seen. Cambodian pediatric students provide the services with supervision by senior staff and multi-national volunteers. There is a warm relationship among the staff and volunteers. As a teacher, I felt rewarded many times over by the eager response to learn and incorporate new information and ideas, and I was honored to be among the first international HVO advisors to receive their Golden Apple Award.

During this period an agreement was signed between AHC and Stony Brook to ensure this student experience would continue indefinitely. However, and quite sadly, this program was unexpectedly phased out in 2010 as a new AHC administration decided to end the Stony Brook resident rotation and shifted interest exclusively to pediatric sub-specialist international volunteers.

While working with the AHC pediatric students, it became apparent that there was little awareness about the need for the regular clinic practice of early diagnosis and intervention. It occurred to me that a simple check list of early developmental milestones for regular use at clinic visits would serve as a reminder and aid in identifying children in need of possible further evaluation and referral. With the assistance of students, a Cambodia Early Developmental Milestones check list was developed and given clinical trials over two consecutive years. It was found to be easily incorporated into the clinic visits and appeared to be effective in identification of children with possible developmental delays or with early-onset developmental disabilities. A paper was published on these trials. The findings were presented in Toronto, Canada at the Pediatric Academic Societies Meeting, as well as in Capetown, South Africa at the International Association for the Scientific Study of Intellectual and Developmental Disabilities meeting, the University of KwaZulu-Natal Medical School in Durban, South Africa, and at the Makerere Medical School in Kampala, Uganda.

The need to identify, as closely as possible, culturally relevant Cambodian developmental milestones for the check list led to a doctoral study by the AHC Chief of Pediatrics, who became greatly interested in early development. His findings were published as a dissertation and will eventually be incorporated into a revised check list. My subsequently published global review study highlighted the limited use of early diagnosis and intervention, especially in low and middle-income countries, and confirmed the need to find ways such as the Cambodia Early Developmental Milestones check list to stimulate this practice.

My part-time clinical patient care and my teaching developmental pediatrics to Stony Brook Residents continued at my Second Street building until 2013 when Stony Brook terminated the lease. Many of us at the clinic felt this was an unjust and unfortunate move as many Riverhead families would now be left without care. I was reassigned to clinic facilities in Hampton Bays and East Moriches, where I became proficient with the electronic medical record (EMR) and continued to enjoy the patient contact and resident teaching. Nevertheless, I became more and more disquieted by the increasing reduction in available time for patients and the demands of mandatory provision of electronic prescriptions.

I had a feeling it was time for me to step down. And so, after five years living overseas, working in the area of international public health education, and fifty years practicing developmental pediatrics, I resigned from Stony Brook in March 2016.

In a long and varied professional career it would be my first time without a medical connection or patient responsibilities. I do continue in my emeritus faculty status at Weill Cornell Medical College and continue my strong affiliation with the American Academy for Cerebral Palsy and Developmental Medicine, where I continue to serve as its historian.

Rather than considering myself as simply retired from further professional activity, I look forward to finding future opportunities where I can hopefully continue to channel some of my interests and energy into further productive responsibilities.

EPILOGUE:
A PERSONAL PERSPECTIVE

Through six US wars and thirteen presidents I have been privileged to roam the world as a health educator and work with children and adults who have disabilities. My fondest dream of becoming a physician was ultimately realized. In retrospect, the ten year hiatus from college to medical school was a blessing in disguise as it enabled me to experience the world and be given in-depth perspectives on South East Asia and the South Pacific, their cultures, history, and politics. I was also able to leave behind in both Burma and Ceylon permanent legacies of extensive national health education programs. In addition, I became academically grounded in both education and sociology, giving me a broad perspective which proved to be critical in defining my field of medicine and the kind of physician I would later become.

The thread of personal failure and inadequacy may have stemmed from the guilt of that summer afternoon with my mother. It then may have grown with the years living with my father and experiencing many psycho-somatic complaints. It may have continued to develop through the years being the overachieving high school nerd, the indifferent college student, and the failed pre-med candidate - a young man zig-zagging between academia and field work, constantly looking to find myself through new experiences. I would overcome all of

125

these challenges with time, persistence, and luck.

And I would do it all over again.
No regrets.
It was worth everything to become a physician.

My early overseas experience has had a very special place in my life. Between Burma and Ceylon and with my regular visits to India, I became comfortably conversant with South East Asia. Little did I visualize how my work in Burma and Ceylon would lead to important national health education programs that are still in existence. The offer to become the WHO regional Health Education Advisor in New Delhi, just as I was about to enter medical school, came at a crucial time indeed. What would have been a cherished prize under other circumstances I quickly dismissed in favor of pursuing a difficult and uncertain medical future. I had no doubts with the P&S acceptance in hand. My later years in Cambodia enabled me to become well acquainted with Thailand, Laos and Vietnam, and broadened my perspective on the entire region.

My hard-won medical school status during the first year was wobbly, to say the least. Other than biochemistry, I struggled mightily in all of my courses, and was saved only by an understanding and helpful faculty. At one point Barbara suggested I give up and admit defeat. I was determined to persevere.

I managed better and better as each year progressed. Perhaps the pedagogic style, strongly emphasizing memorization then in vogue, was a factor in my difficulty in learning the first year or two. Had we used today's methods of references, problem-solving, and clinical correlation, it might have been very different. However, it all came together when focus was placed on the patient. I never missed our five year anniversary reunions and was emotionally drained at the fiftieth, finding it difficult to truly comprehend the rush of years since we had all started off down this road.

My choice of pediatrics as my specialization was interesting. The quest to become a physician had been a part of me as long as I could remember, perhaps the origins go back to that unhappy summer afternoon when I failed my mother. Or perhaps it was even earlier when I had first become aware of her illness. Whatever the root, though, the interest had never really been specific. The push to become a doctor had led me to unsuccessfully seek early admission (i.e. after only three years of college) at McGill University in Montreal, where a branch of the Scherzer family was supportive and helpful. I don't remember being more specific on any of my initial or subsequent applications. Possibly it was immaturity or self-doubt. The idea of becoming a public health physician never occurred to me during that graduate year, but struck me as what could be a possible goal when I later visited American Samoa. Perhaps this was what I had had in mind when I started medical school.

Struggling through basic sciences in the first and second years of medical school left little time or energy to consider my medical future. Third year rotation in pediatrics whetted my interest, but it was not until early in the fourth year in clinical pediatrics that I made the choice. I realized that pediatrics would enable me to maintain the clinical knowledge and skills I had achieved with so much effort. By then, it had also become apparent that my earlier thought of specialization in preventive medicine and public health was likely to lead to becoming an administrator and divert me from involvement with clinical care. I would have preferred to stay on at Columbia Presbyterian Hospital for my year of pediatric internship but this was not offered at that time and I matched to Cornell. I had a choice of returning to Columbia for my two years of pediatric residency but

127

decided to stay on at Cornell since I was quite satisfied with the faculty and program and wanted to avoid disrupting my family. As it turned out, the choice to stay on at Cornell for my residency virtually changed our lives.

My future pediatric commitment enfolded as I became acquainted with cerebral palsy, the CP Clinic at the Hospital for Special Surgery, and Dr. Cooper. I was startled to realize that my education at one of the most highly regarded US medical schools never exposed me to the child with cerebral palsy or any other physical disabilities. That first contact immediately enabled me to envision a way to meld clinical medicine, education, and my sociological background in dealing with the family. The connection with Bill Cooper eventually moved this new interest to a joint position between Cornell and the Nassau CP Center and thus became the start of my career. I never seriously entertained the alternatives of general pediatrics practice, or going on for more fellowship training, perhaps in neurology. At the time, I understood that no formal preparation was available in this field and that clinical experience supplemented by additional lectures and courses would gradually provide my training. In those days the need to become a trained pediatric sub-specialist was not considered to be critical since it was common for general pediatricians to confine their professional interest to a particular area without formal specialization. As it turned out, the Instructional Courses at annual meetings of the American Academy for Cerebral Palsy and Developmental Medicine regularly provided as much "formal" training as I would ever have and enabled me to become a significant part of this developing field. That I had not even been exposed to the child with disabilities until my residency years at Cornell was a serious flaw in my basic medical education and remains a challenge needed to be faced at some US medical schools - even today.

After fifty years in clinical developmental pediatrics practice, I have been able to experience the broad range of its evolution from major focus on motor disabilities like cerebral palsy to more recent inclusion of behavioral and cognitive disorders. Along the way, I have been observer, practitioner, and, at times, critic of the evolving approaches to training and treatment. Although I was able to practice in my day with only a special interest, a general pediatric background, and learning as I went along, required specialized training has now become the norm. Two sub-specialty training approaches have evolved - neuro-developmental pediatrics, and developmental-behavioral pediatrics. In my view, neither is able to provide for a sufficiently broad approach. The former emphasizes neurology and the physically disabled child, while the latter focuses on psychiatry and the child with behavioral/learning problems. There are major gaps in each with little emphasis given to training in the relevant field of education which I have found to be essential in care and management. Future revision and amalgamation of these two available channels for training is essential for this field to move forward and produce well-rounded specialists in Developmental Pediatrics.

Over the years, I have also been able to observe important positive changes in the field of childhood disability. Beginning in the '70s, enactment of legislation in the US mandating education of all children irrespective of disability has increasingly provided a stable foundation for future development. Federal legislation has also greatly improved environmental street and building design, enhancing mobility and accessibility. And the WHO International Classification of Functioning, Disability, and Health (ICF) now provides uniform guidelines for assessment of function and planning for needed services.

However, I am particularly concerned about two areas

129

where positive change in this field has been either inadequate or non-existent. In low and middle-income countries of the world there has been a recent reduction of childhood mortality under age five and increasing childhood developmental delays and disabilities. Yet there is insufficient sensitivity to this rapidly enlarging childhood population and limited availability of early diagnosis and appropriate intervention for these children. Alerting and stimulating action by UN agencies, governments, foundations, and non-governmental agencies (NGOs) is a major international need that must lead to substantial direction and funding now. Another serious gap is the lack of public understanding, social acceptance, and persistent prejudice toward people with disabilities. This continues to affect social integration, higher education, employment, and housing. Obviously much remains to be done in this important area of civil rights through education and effective leadership.

In the final analysis we need a better understanding of the childhood behavioral disorders, the causes of childhood onset disability, and the best approaches to care and management. When I first started in 1966, dramatic improvement in cerebral palsy was reported solely on the basis of purely anecdotal reports of various discrete systems of therapy. Today, sophisticated computerized research is enabling a clearer understanding of causation and more effective methods of care. Continued expansion of larger and more inclusive studies is clearly needed to keep up with rapid developments in the field.

A happy consequence of my longevity has been observing both the shrinking of our planet and the interdependence this has evoked. This phenomenon has extended to the world of children with developmental disabilities. Originally initiated in 1946 as an exclusive private club for specialists in the field, the American Academy for Cerebral Palsy and Developmental Medicine has evolved to become a model for similar organizations around the world as international communication and professional interchange has increased. Comparable organizations now exist in Europe, Australasia, India, with ones developing in Mexico and Africa. The growing strength of these groups has led to the formation of the International Alliance of Academies for Childhood Disabilities (IAACD) which had its first joint meeting in Stockholm, Sweden in 2016. Joint meetings are planned for different world regions every three years with the next scheduled for Anaheim, California in 2019. It is hoped that the growth and interaction of these organizations will lead to improved regional awareness, early diagnosis, meaningful intervention, and long term care facilities, especially in areas where services are limited or non-existent. This achievement of international focus in the field of childhood disability during my lifetime is yet another reason for me to be grateful for the opportunity I have been afforded to participate.

ACKNOWLEDGMENTS

I began writing personal sketches about my life soon after retiring from Cornell in 1994 without any serious ambitions toward eventual publication. Progress was slow and intermittent. My efforts petered out entirely when Barbara died in 2003. However, time for reflection became abundantly available following my retirement in March 2016, and turning to my files, I discovered long-forgotten extensive notes and comments about the sketches made by Martha, my youngest daughter. I am very grateful to Martha, herself a serious writer, for helping me to return to this project and bring it up-to-date.

I naturally turned to Mary Randall, another fine writer and Martha's close friend, for comments on the manuscript. I want to thank her for quickly setting me on the right direction.

CITATION TO DR. SCHERZER UPON RECEIVING
THE 2006 HEALTH VOLUNTEERS OVERSEAS
GOLDEN APPLE AWARD

...(Dr. Scherzer) was selected for this recognition for his work with the HVO pediatric training program in Cambodia at the Angkor Hospital for Children (AHC). Over the past two years Dr. Scherzer has made three volunteer trips to the program. On his initial trip he recognized the glaring need for training in developmental disability identification and management at the hospital. As a result, he has established training workshops for the hospital staff and for the ancillary personnel at associated country-side clinics. In addition, he has helped to revise neurology forms and developmental assessment records as well as developing a Khmer language questionnaire to assess awareness of disabilities. Dr. Scherzer is commended for his many efforts at AHC by all of the hospital staff and the program director who nominated him for this award. The program director remarks, "Dr. Scherzer has been an exceptional resource for this new hospital and his enthusiasm for his specialty has been contagious."